Ravenscourt
B·O·O·K·S
Teacher's Guide

Getting Started
Books 1-8

Let's Go Camping
Baseball
You Are Not Green
The Pond
Freedom Morning
The Fox and the Hen
The Farm
Log Cabin Help

Columbus, OH

SRAonline.com

 SRA

Copyright © 2008 by SRA/McGraw-Hill.

All rights reserved. No part of this publication may be reproduced or distributed in any form or by any means, or stored in a database or retrieval system, without the prior written consent of The McGraw-Hill Companies, Inc., including, but not limited to, network storage or transmission, or broadcast for distance learning.

Printed in the United States of America.

Send all inquiries to this address:
SRA/McGraw-Hill
4400 Easton Commons
Columbus, OH 43219

ISBN: 978-0-07-611310-1
MHID: 0-07-611310-8

4 5 6 7 8 9 MAL 13 12 11 10

Table of Contents

Ravenscourt Books 1
Reading and Fluency 2
Using *Ravenscourt Books* 3
Individual Progress Chart 8
Fluency Graph 9
Book Summaries 10
Let's Go Camping 12
    Answer Key 22
Baseball 24
    Answer Key 34
You Are Not Green 36
    Answer Key 46
The Pond 48
    Answer Key 58
Freedom Morning 60
    Answer Key 70
The Fox and the Hen 72
    Answer Key 82
The Farm 84
    Answer Key 94
Log Cabin Help 96
    Answer Key 106
Graphic Organizers 108

Ravenscourt Books

Placing Students

Written for middle school to young adult readers, **Ravenscourt Books** provides materials and activities for enhancing the comprehension and fluency of struggling readers. Each of these fiction and nonfiction selections is

- organized within themes that are both engaging and informative.
- built to provide students with additional opportunities to read independently.
- designed to provide frequent opportunities for reading to improve fluency and overall reading achievement.

Some teachers have found these selections align with the independent reading levels of students in the **Corrective Reading** program. Use the chart below to place your students in the appropriate set of **Ravenscourt Readers.**

	For students who have successfully completed	Reading level	Page count (average number of words per book)
Getting Started	Corrective Reading Decoding A*	1	28 (800)
Discovery	Corrective Reading Comprehension A*	2	28 (1,800)
Anything's Possible	Corrective Reading Decoding B1*	2	28 (1,800)
The Unexpected	Corrective Reading Comprehension B1*	2	28 (1,800)
Express Yourself	Corrective Reading Decoding B2*	3	44 (4,200)
Overcoming Adversity	Corrective Reading Comprehension B2*	3	44 (4,200)
Moving Forward	Corrective Reading Decoding C* Lesson 60	5	60 (7,500)
Reaching Goals	Corrective Reading Comprehension C* Lesson 60	5	60 (7,500)

*or have attained comparable skills

Components

The **Using Ravenscourt Books** section explains how to incorporate these components into an effective supplemental reading program.

Chapter Books
- Include eight age-appropriate books in each set
- Feature fiction, nonfiction, and retold classics
- Present additional practice for essential vocabulary and decoding skills
- Provide fast-moving story lines for independent reading

Fluency Audio CDs
- Model pronunciation, phrasing, intonation, and expression
- Assist students in improving their oral-reading fluency

Evaluation and Tracking Software
- Motivates students by delivering activities electronically
- Scores, records, and tracks student progress

Teacher's Guides
- Outline ways to use the series in your classroom
- Include comprehension activities, word lists, and fluency practice
- Provide prereading activities and postreading writing activities
- Address reading and language arts standards

Online Support

Go to **SRAonline.com** and click on **Ravenscourt Books** for additional support and materials.

Reading and Fluency

Reading

Reading is not simply decoding or word recognition; it is understanding the text. Students who read slowly or hesitantly are not able to concentrate on meaning.

Fluency

Fluency bridges the gap between decoding and comprehension and characterizes proficient reading. Increased oral-reading fluency improves reading comprehension.

Fluent and Nonfluent Readers

The chart below presents an easy way to compare fluent and nonfluent readers. If students have several of the listed characteristics of nonfluent readers, refer to the sections on *Assessing Fluency* and *Fluency Practice* in the **Using *Ravenscourt Books*** section that begins on page 3.

A Fluent Reader	A Nonfluent Reader
Reads words accurately	Reads with omissions, pauses, mispronunciations, insertions, and substitutions
Decodes automatically	Reverses word order
Reads smoothly	Reads word-by-word, focusing on words
Reads at an appropriate rate	Reads slowly, hesitantly
Reads with expression and phrasing	Reads without expression; ignores punctuation
Reads with understanding of text	Reads with limited comprehension
Reads so text sounds like speech	Reads without natural intonation

Oral-Reading Fluency

Oral-reading fluency is the ability to read accurately, at an appropriate rate, and with good expression and phrasing. The foundation for oral-reading fluency is automatic word recognition and extensive practice with materials that are easy for the students to read.

Oral-reading fluency develops as a result of multiple opportunities to practice reading successfully. The primary strategy for developing oral-reading fluency is to provide extensive and frequent opportunities for students to read text with high levels of accuracy. This means that selected passages should be ones the students are able to read with at least 95 percent accuracy.

Repeated and monitored oral reading is an effective intervention strategy for students who do not read fluently. By reading the same passage a number of times, students become familiar with the words it contains and recognize the words automatically. This improves reading fluency and overall reading achievement. It also builds confidence and motivation—particularly when students chart their progress.

The minimum target oral-reading fluency rate is 60 *words read correctly per minute* (wcpm) for **Getting Started** and **Discovery,** 90 wcpm for **Anything's Possible** and **The Unexpected,** 130 wcpm for **Express Yourself** and **Overcoming Adversity,** and 150 wcpm for **Moving Forward** and **Reaching Goals.**

How to assess fluency, how to set realistic target rates, and how to practice fluency will be discussed in greater detail in the **Using *Ravenscourt Books*** section.

Using Ravenscourt Books

Grouping

Students who have completed *Decoding A* will have mastered the decoding skills and vocabulary necessary to independently read the stories in **Getting Started.**

Ravenscourt Books may be taught to the whole class, small groups, or pairs. Assign each student to a partner. Partners can do paired readings for fluency practice. The partners will read the same story at the same time. *Ravenscourt Books* may also be used for individual student reading.

Scheduling

Ravenscourt Books is intended to be used as a supplement to your core program and should be scheduled in addition to the regular lessons. Times to use the books include

- reading and language arts blocks,
- before- and after-school programs,
- summer school,
- and out-of-school reading with parental support.

	A Suggested Lesson Plan for *Ravenscourt Books*
Part 1	1) Introduce the series, and help students select a book. 2) Assess students' initial oral-reading fluency by completing a "cold read" of one of the book's fluency passages. The **Fluency Passage** section can be found after the **Thinking and Writing** section for each book. (See *Assessing Fluency* on page 4.) 3) Have students complete the **Building Background** activities.
Part 2	1) Preteach the unfamiliar words for the first chapter in the **Word Lists** section of the *Teacher's Guide* for each book. 2) Have students read the title of the first chapter aloud. 3) Have students listen to a fluent reader read the first chapter as they follow along with the text. 4) Have student pairs take turns reading the chapter again. 5) Have students take the **Chapter Quiz.** 6) Have some students do repeated readings to improve oral-reading fluency. 7) Repeat Part 2 for subsequent chapters.
Part 3	1) Have students complete the **Thinking and Writing** section. 2) Take fluency scores, using the same fluency passage used in Part 1. Have students enter their scores on their **Fluency Graph.**

Selecting Books

The books in each set are leveled so students can start with any book in the set. However, students generally find contemporary fiction easier to read than nonfiction and retold classics.

On pages 10–11 you will find **Book Summaries** that give a brief outline of each book.

- If the book is a retold classic, information about the original author is included.
- If the book is a good tool for teaching a literary term, the term is explained. The teacher should teach the term before the students begin reading.
- The last section includes other resources—books, films, or Web sites—that contain related information. These resources can be used for extra credit, reports, projects, and so on. Evaluate all books, films, and Web sites to confirm appropriateness of the content prior to sharing these materials with students.

Using Ravenscourt Books

Introducing the Series

1. Write the series theme on the board.
   - Tell the students that the books in the set all relate in some way to this common theme.
   - Brainstorm ideas about the theme, and write the students' ideas on a large sheet of chart paper. Include words, topics, and types of stories related to the theme. Post this list for student reference.
2. The books in each set represent several genres—fiction, nonfiction, biography, science fiction, historical fiction, retold classics, and so on.
   - Ask the students to read the title and the summary on the back of the book they chose.
   - Have the students predict how their book relates to the theme.
   - If the book is nonfiction, ask the student to predict what kinds of questions it could answer.

Whole-Class Instruction

The following sections are designed for whole-class instruction but may be modified for small groups or individual instruction.

Set up classes in the *Evaluation and Tracking Software,* or make a copy of the **Individual Progress Chart** for each student.

Assessing Fluency

Make a class set of copies of the **Fluency Graph** on page 9 of the *Teacher's Guide.* Follow these steps to **ASSESS STUDENTS' INITIAL ORAL-READING FLUENCY.**

1. Have the student read a passage that is set at the appropriate length (60–150 words) and at the appropriate instructional reading level (at least 95 percent accuracy).
   - The **Fluency Passage** section can be found after the **Thinking and Writing** section for each book.
2. Ask the student to do a one-minute reading of the unrehearsed passage.
3. Ask the student whether she or he is ready.
   - Then say: **Please begin.**
4. Follow along as the student reads.
   - When an error occurs, mark the error.
   - Count the following as errors: mispronunciations, omissions, substitutions, insertions, and failure to identify a word within three seconds.
   - Don't mark words the student self-corrects.
   - Don't mark off for proper nouns.
5. At the end of one minute, make a vertical line on the page after the last word read.
6. Count the number of words up to the last word read.
7. Subtract the number of errors to determine the wcpm.
8. Enter the number of words read correctly on the student's **Fluency Graph** by filling in the column to the appropriate number.
9. At the bottom of the graph, circle the number of errors made.
10. Review any words the student missed and provide practice on those words. The minimum goals for fluency are the following:
    - The goal for students who have completed *Decoding A* or have equivalent skills is to read the books in **Getting Started** at a minimum rate of 60 wcpm.
    - The goal for students who have completed *Comprehension A* or have equivalent skills is to read the books in **Discovery** at a minimum rate of 60 wcpm.
    - The goal for students who have completed *Decoding B1* or have equivalent skills is to read the books in **Anything's Possible** at a minimum rate of 90 wcpm.
    - The goal for students who have completed *Comprehension B1* or have equivalent skills is to read the books in **The Unexpected** at a minimum rate of 90 wcpm.

Using Ravenscourt Books

- The goal for students who have completed *Decoding B2* or have equivalent skills is to read the books in **Express Yourself** at a minimum rate of 130 wcpm.
- The goal for students who have completed *Comprehension B2* or have equivalent skills is to read the books in **Overcoming Adversity** at a minimum rate of 130 wcpm.
- The goal for students who have completed Lesson 60 of *Decoding C* or have equivalent skills is to read the books in **Moving Forward** at a minimum rate of 150 wcpm.
- The goal for students who have completed Lesson 60 of *Comprehension C* or have equivalent skills is to read the books in **Reaching Goals** at a minimum rate of 150 wcpm.

Word Lists

Follow this procedure to preteach the words for each chapter of every book.

1. Provide students with a copy of the **Word Lists** page, or copy the words onto the board. Underline word parts if appropriate.
2. Begin with *Proper Nouns* by saying:
   - **These are the names of important people and places in Chapter 1.**
   - **Touch the first word in the column.**
   - Point to an underlined word part (if necessary) and say: **What sound?** (Signal.)
   - **What word?** (Signal.)
   - (Repeat until firm.)
3. For difficult and irregular words, say:
   - **Touch the word.**
   - **The word is ____.** (Signal.)
   - **What word?** (Signal.)
   - **Spell ____.** (Signal for each letter.)
   - **What word?** (Signal.)
   - (Repeat until firm.)
4. Follow the same procedure with *Unfamiliar Words*. Discuss the meanings of the words. Use the words in sentences as needed. The *Word Meanings* category is comprised of the words used in the *Word Meanings* section of **Building Background,** so some of the words may be familiar. Only use the following procedure for unfamiliar words.
   - Point to each unfamiliar word, say the word, and then say **What does ____ mean?** (Call on individual students.)
   - (Repeat until firm.)

Building Background

Use the **Building Background** section in the *Teacher's Guide* or on the *Evaluation and Tracking Software*. You can use this section as a whole-class activity or as an independent activity.

Whole-Class Activity

1. Divide the students into small groups. Hand out copies of the **Building Background** page for that book.
2. Read the questions in the *What You Know* section. Have the groups discuss the questions and write an answer for them. Have a member of each group read the group's answers to the class.
3. Read the words in the *Word Meanings* section.
   - Then read the directions and go over each question with the students and say, **Which word best answers this question?** (Call on individual students.)
   - Repeat this procedure for all of the words. (Note: If the directions indicate that the questions should be answered once the words have been introduced in the book, go over each word again after the students have read the word in context and have them answer the question associated with that word.)
4. Collect the papers and score them based on the number of correct answers. Refer to the **Answer Key** for each book.

Using *Ravenscourt* Books

Independent Activity

1. Hand out copies of the **Building Background** page. Have students take turns reading each question in the *What You Know* section. Have students write their answers before proceeding to the next question.
2. Have students read the words in the *Word Meanings* section. Then have them read the directions and complete the section.
   - When students are finished, collect the papers and score them based on completion and effort. Refer to the **Answer Key** for each book.

The teacher may enter the scores on the **Individual Progress Chart** found in the *Teacher's Guide* or on the *Evaluation and Tracking Software.*

Reading the Chapter

First, the students listen to a fluent reader read the chapter. The fluency model may be the teacher, a parent, a tutor, a teacher's aide, a peer, or the *Fluency Audio CDs.* Students read along, tracking the text with their fingers. Next, students take turns reading the chapter with their peer partner. An individual student reads aloud to the teacher, tutor, or parent, who gives feedback, points out missed words, and models, using punctuation, to improve expressive reading.

Chapter Quiz

After the second reading of the chapter, the student takes the **Chapter Quiz.** The quizzes have multiple-choice, true-or-false, sequence, and short-answer questions. The chapter quizzes are available on the *Evaluation and Tracking Software* or as blackline masters in the *Teacher's Guide.* Use the **Answer Keys** to score the blackline masters and enter scores on the **Individual Progress Chart** found on page 8. The *Evaluation and Tracking Software* will automatically grade and record the scores for all non-short-answer questions for each **Chapter Quiz.**

Students should take each quiz once and do their best the first time. Students must score a minimum of 80 percent to continue. If the student does not score 80 percent, he or she should reread the chapter before retaking the quiz.

Fluency Practice

Fluency practice improves comprehension. The teacher may choose different ways to practice fluency, depending on the student's needs. For students who are close to the target rate, have the student reread the whole chapter using one of these techniques:

- **Echo reading** A fluent reader reads a sentence aloud, and the student *echoes* it—repeats it with the same intonation and phrasing.
- **Unison or choral reading** A pair, group, or class reads a chapter aloud together.
- **Paired reading** The student reads a page aloud and receives feedback from his or her peer partner. Record the fluency scores on the **Fluency Graph** found in the *Teacher's Guide* or on the *Evaluation and Tracking Software.* Recording progress motivates student achievement.

For students who are significantly below the target rate, conduct **REPEATED READINGS TO IMPROVE ORAL-READING FLUENCY.** The student will reread the passages marked by asterisks in each of the books' chapters.

1. Set a target rate for the passage.
   - The target rate should be high enough to require the student to reread the passage several times.
   - A reasonable target rate is 40 percent higher than the baseline level.
   - For example, if the student initially reads the passage at a rate of 60 wcpm, the target rate for that passage would be 84 wcpm (**60** x .40 = 24; **60** + 24 = 84).

Using Ravenscourt Books

2. Have the student listen to the passage read fluently by a skilled reader or on the corresponding *Fluency Audio CD* while following along, pointing to the words as they are read.
3. After listening to the fluency model, have the student rereads the same passage aloud for one minute.
   - A partner listens and records errors but does not interrupt the reader during the one-minute timed reading.
   - If the student makes more than six errors, he or she should listen to the fluency model again.
4. The student should read the same passage three to five times during the session or until the target rate is met, whichever comes first.
   - After each rereading, the student records the wcpm on his or her **Fluency Graph.**
   - If the target rate is not met, have the student read the same passage again the next day.
   - If the target rate is met, the student repeats the procedure with the next chapter.

Thinking and Writing

Many state assessments require students to produce extended writing about a story or an article they have read. Like **Building Background,** this section is not computer-scored and may be used in one of several ways. The *Think About It* section is intended to help students summarize what they have read and to relate the book to other books in the set, to the theme, or to the students' life experiences.

1. The questions in the *Think About It* section can be used for discussion.
   - Students discuss the questions in small groups and then write their individual responses on the blackline masters or using the *Evaluation and Tracking Software.*
   - The teacher may score the response using a variety of rubrics. For example, the teacher could give points for all reasonable responses in complete sentences that begin with a capital letter and end with appropriate punctuation.
2. For certain students, the teacher may ask the questions and prompt the student to give a thoughtful oral response.
3. Another option is to use *Think About It* as a mini-assessment. Have the students answer the questions independently on paper or using the *Evaluation and Tracking Software.*

The *Write About It* section gives students extended practice writing about what they have read. Students may write for as long as time allows.

The students may answer on the blackline master or use the *Evaluation and Tracking Software.* To motivate students, the *Evaluation and Tracking Software* includes a spelling checker and a variety of fonts and colors for students to choose from. This section is teacher-scored. Scores may be entered on a copy of the **Individual Progress Chart** or on the *Evaluation and Tracking Software.*

Students may keep their essays in a writing portfolio. At the end of the term students choose one of their essays to improve using the writing process. The final question in each *Write About It* section asks students to complete one of the graphic organizers that can be found as blackline masters in the back of this *Teacher's Guide* or on the *Evaluation and Tracking Software.* Graphic organizers are a structured, alternative writing experience. There are Book Report Forms, a What I Know/What I Learned Chart, a Sequencing Chart, and so on. Scores may be entered on the blackline master or *Evaluation and Tracking Software* version of the **Individual Progress Chart.**

Individual Progress Chart

- Enter the percentage correct score for each quiz or activity.

Book Title	Building Background	Chapter 1 Quiz	Chapter 2 Quiz	Chapter 3 Quiz	Chapter 4 Quiz	Chapter 5 Quiz	Chapter 6 Quiz	Thinking and Writing	Graphic Organizer
Let's Go Camping									
Baseball									
You Are Not Green									
The Pond									
Freedom Morning									
The Fox and the Hen									
The Farm									
Log Cabin Help									

Name: _____ Class: _____

Fluency Graph

Name: _____ Class: _____

WCPM RATE
Number of words read correctly in one minute

Vertical axis values: 10, 20, 30, 40, 50, 60, 70, 80, 90, 100, 110, 120, 130, 140, 150, 160, 170, 180

Date | ERRORS (0, 1, 2, 3, 4, 5, 6, Above 6)

1. Read a fluency passage for one minute. 2. Find the next open column. 3. Color the column to the number that shows how far you read. 4. Mark the number of errors in the chart at the bottom.

Getting Started

Book Summaries

Let's Go Camping
By Nancy J. Nielsen

Summary
In this adventure story, told in the first person, Dad, Mom, two children, and the dog go camping at the lake. The family members work together to get ready, pack the van, and set up camp when they arrive. They take a family hike, swim in the lake, and fish. When ants ruin the dinner ham, they enjoy corn hash and fish instead.

Literary Terms
Fiction: a piece of literature that is invented
Setting: the story environment; its time and place

Other Resources
Books: O'Connell, Kristine and George and Kate Kiesler. *Toasting Marshmallows: Camping Poems* (Clarion Books, 2001); Ruurs, Margriet and Andrew Kiss. *When We Go Camping* (Tundra Books, 2001)

Movies: *The Beginners Guide to Camping* (2004); *Camp Nowhere* (1994)

Web site: http://www.multiage-education.com/multiagelessons/camping/campingprocess.html

Baseball
By Nancy J. Nielsen

Summary
Sid and Al join Bud's Red Team. After practicing, the Red Team begins to play other teams. They lose one game to the Green Team, but win other games. When they play the Green Team again, they win and become the champions.

Literary Terms
Plot: sequence of events with rising action, conflict, climax, and resolution
Dialogue: the words spoken by characters in a story

Other Resources
Book: Ritter, John H. *The Boy Who Saved Baseball* (Puffin; Reprint edition, 2005)

Movies: *The Rookie* (2002); *Air Bud: Seventh Inning Fetch* (2002)

Web sites: http://www.northcanton.sparcc.org/~greentown/webquests/baseball/bballwebq.htm
http://www.webquests.ips.k12.in.us/Communities/webquests/Assets/webquests/68/la/spring02/raney/WebQuest.htm

You Are Not Green
By Linda Barr

Summary
Duck wants to be Frog's friend, but Frog believes he can only be friends with other frogs. Since Duck is not green and cold, Frog will not be his friend. But when a hawk grabs Frog from the pond and drops him on a hill, Frog becomes injured and lost. He cannot get back to the pond, and he cannot stay wet. Duck rescues Frog and flies him back to the pond. Frog discovers that differences are strengths, and that Duck can be his friend.

Literary Terms
Suspense: arousing the reader's curiosity or making the reader wonder what will happen next
Moral: the lesson a story teaches or implies

Other Resources
Books: Timbers, James. *Salmon and Fuzz in Helping a Friend* (PublishAmerica, 2005); Hatkoff, Craig and Peter Greste. *Owen & Mzee: The True Story Of A Remarkable Friendship* (Scholastic Press, 2006)

Movies: *Babe: Pig in the City* (1998); *Frog and Toad Are Friends* (1993)

Web site: http://www.catawba.k12.nc.us/techtrac/plus/simmons/

The Pond
By Nancy J. Nielsen

Summary
The Pond explores the ecosystem of a pond in the winter and spring. Readers learn about different pond dwellers and their relationship to other various pond dwellers. Ducks, fish, beavers, rats, frogs, and bugs are some of the animals that live in a pond environment. One of the main ideas the book discusses is the cyclical interdependence of pond, plant, and animal life. One example is that frogs attach their eggs to the plants in the water. Water bugs and fish then feed on the eggs.

Literary Term
Nonfiction: a factual piece of literature

Other Resources
Book: Stewart, David, Carolyn Scrace, and Mark Bergin. *Pond Life (Cycles of Life)* (Franklin Watts, 2002)

Movies: *National Geographic: Really Wild Animals—Totally Tropical Rain Forest* (1994); *ABC of the Animal World* (1994)

Web site: http://www.naturegrid.org.uk/pondexplorer/pondexplorer.html

Book Summaries

Freedom Morning
By Kathleen Thompson

Summary

Set during the U.S. Civil War, Sally, a young African American girl, agrees to deliver a basket of eggs to a local farmer. Hidden among the eggs is a hollow egg that contains a letter outlining the plans of the Southern army. The plans came from a spy working for Jefferson Davis. Despite being afraid, Sally agrees to do the job as part of the effort to obtain freedom for African Americans. After being stopped by a guard, Sally successfully delivers the egg to an agent of the North.

Literary Terms

Plot: sequence of events with rising action, conflict, climax, and resolution

Suspense: arousing the reader's curiosity or making the reader wonder what will happen next

Setting: the story environment; its time and place

Other Resources

Books: Coles, Robert and George Ford. *The Story of Ruby Bridges* (Scholastic Press, 1995); Bridges, Ruby. *Through My Eyes* (Scholastic Press, 1999)

Movie: *Ruby Bridges* (1998)

Web sites: http://www.42explore2.com/undergrd.htm
http://www.narragansett.k12.ri.us/Nes/Undergroundrailroad.html

The Fox and the Hen
By Nancy J. Nielsen

Summary

This is a story about Fox and Hen. Fox wants to eat Hen, so he tells his mother to boil a pot of water in which to cook Hen. Fox then hides in Hen's shed. When Hen returns, he captures her in a sack. On the way home to his den, Fox stops to rest. While Fox is sleeping, Hen escapes and puts a rock in the sack. Then Hen uses her sewing kit to repair the sack. When Fox arrives at his den, he dumps the rock into the boiling water, which splashes on Fox and his mother. The foxes go to bed without dinner, and Hen is happy to be safe.

Literary Terms

Plot: sequence of events with rising action, conflict, climax, and resolution

Moral: the lesson a story teaches or implies

Other Resources

Books: Moore, Beth and Beverly Warren. *A Parable About the King* (B&H Publishing Group, 2003); Bishop, Jennie and Preston McDaniels. *The Squire and the Scroll* (Warner Press, 2004)

Movies: *The Princess and the Pea* (1976); *The Tale of The Frog Prince* (1982)

The Farm
By Nancy J. Nielsen

Summary

This book describes a farm and the people and animals who live and work there. The farm has a lot of land and different kinds of animals and crops. There are pigs, cows, sheep, horses, and hens. Some of the animals are sold and some have babies. Farm hands help the dad with the work. The boy and girl help, too, and have fun doing so. Everyone enjoys working on the farm.

Literary Term

Setting: the story environment; its time and place

Other Resources

Book: Provensen, Alice and Martin Provensen. *Our Animal Friends at Maple Hill Farm.* (Aladdin; Reprint edition, 2001)

Movies: *Chicken Run* (2000); *Home on the Range* (2004)

Web sites: http://web2.airmail.net/bealke/
http://42explore.com/farming.htm

Log Cabin Help
By Nancy J. Nielsen

Summary

Dan, Ted, and Ann are siblings who live in a log cabin with their mom and dad. They go to a one-room schoolhouse. They help their parents with chores, such as cooking, setting traps, and chopping wood. One night it snows. The children take their sled to school. On the way home, Ted rides the sled down a steep hill and crashes into a tree. Ted hurts his leg, so Dan and Ann put Ted on the sled and take him home. Ted rests at home and gets better.

Literary Terms

Dialogue: the words spoken by characters in a story

Setting: the story environment; its time and place

Other Resources

Books: Ingalls Wilder, Laura and Doris Ettlinger. *Sugar Snow (My First Little House)* (HarperTrophy; New Ed edition, 1999); Ingalls Wilder, Laura and Jody Wheeler. *Winter on the Farm (My First Little House)* (HarperTrophy; New Ed edition, 1999)

Web site: http://www.museum.state.il.us/exhibits/athome/1800/objects/1furniture.htm

Building Background

Name _____ Date _____

Let's Go Camping
What You Know

Write answers to these questions.

1. What is something fun you and your family do? _____
   _____
   _____

2. Think of two things you need to take with you if you go camping.
   _____
   _____

Word Meanings
Definitions

Look for these words as you read your chapter book. When you find one of these words, write its definition.

dock: _____

eat: _____

fire: _____

hash: _____

lake: _____

look: _____

Word Lists

Let's Go Camping

Unfamiliar Words	Word Meanings	
puts says too	lake	Chapter 1
wood	fire	Chapter 2
off some where	look	Chapter 3
water	dock	Chapter 4
makes say want	eat hash	Chapter 5
	like	Chapter 6

Getting Started • Book 1

Chapter Quiz

Name _____ Date _____

Let's Go Camping
Chapter 1, "Let's Go Camping"

Mark each statement *T* for true or *F* for false.

_____ 1. There are four people in this family.

_____ 2. Mom puts bags in the van.

_____ 3. The dog's name is Ann.

_____ 4. The dog is not going camping.

_____ 5. They go north to the lake.

Read the question, and write your answer.

Why does Dad want to go camping? _____

_____

Chapter Quiz

Name _____ Date _____

Let's Go Camping
Chapter 2, "At the Camp"

Fill in the bubble beside the answer for each question.

1. Who sets up the tent?
   - Ⓐ Mom and Dad
   - Ⓑ Dad
   - Ⓒ Mom and Ann

2. A bug gets
   - Ⓐ Dad.
   - Ⓑ Ann.
   - Ⓒ Mom.

3. What does Dad want to do?
   - Ⓐ go for a walk
   - Ⓑ sleep
   - Ⓒ sit by the fire pit

Chapter Quiz

Name _____ Date _____

Let's Go Camping
Chapter 3, "The Path"

Number the events in order from 1 to 5.

____ Dad says, "We can go down the path."

____ Bud gets muddy.

____ Mom asks, "What did he do that for?"

____ Ann sees a path.

____ Bud rubs his neck in the mud.

Chapter Quiz

Name _____ Date _____

Let's Go Camping
Chapter 4, "Swimming"

Number the events in order from 1 to 5.

___ Bud slips on the dock.

___ Ann says, "Let's go swimming!"

___ Ann picks up a shell and puts it in her vest.

___ Bud swims to the shore.

___ Bud runs on the dock.

Read the question, and write your answer.

Why is Bud not muddy now? _____

_____

Chapter Quiz

Name _____ Date _____

Let's Go Camping
Chapter 5, "Corn Hash"

Fill in the bubble beside the answer for each question.

1. Who went fishing?
   - Ⓐ Dad
   - Ⓑ Dad and Ann
   - Ⓒ Mom and Dad

2. Why don't they eat the ham?
   - Ⓐ It is not cooked.
   - Ⓑ Bud has eaten half of it already.
   - Ⓒ It has ants on it.

3. What does Mom make for dinner?
   - Ⓐ sandwiches
   - Ⓑ soup
   - Ⓒ corn hash

Read the question, and write your answer.

Who eats the ham? _____

Chapter Quiz

Name _____ Date _____

Let's Go Camping
Chapter 6, "Dinner at Last!"

Mark each statement *T* for true or *F* for false.

___ 1. Mom says it is okay to eat before Dad and Ann get back.

___ 2. Dad and Ann bring fish.

___ 3. The family eats ham and corn hash for dinner.

___ 4. The sun sets.

___ 5. The family did not have fun camping.

Thinking and Writing

Name _____ Date _____

Let's Go Camping
Think About It

Write about or give an oral presentation for each question.

1. What part of this camping trip do you think was the most fun?

   _____

   _____

   _____

2. What is a fun place you go with your family? Why is it fun?

   _____

   _____

   _____

Write About It

Choose one of the questions below. Write your answer on a sheet of paper.

1. If you could take a trip anywhere, where would you go?

2. Complete the Sequencing Chart for this book.

Fluency Passages

Let's Go Camping

Chapter 2 *page 7*

*"Let's get wood," Dad says. "We need wood for a fire."	11
The land has a lot of wood on it. Dad and I pick up a lot of wood. Dad	30
puts it by the fire pit.	36
Then Dad drops the wood on a stump. *Chop! Chop!* He chops the	49
wood.	50
"Now we can camp," Dad says. "I will sit by* the fire pit."	63

Chapter 6 *pages 24 and 25*

*I have a fork. I have a glass. I have a dish. I want to eat.	16
When will Dad and Ann be back?	23
Just then I see Dad and Ann. They are on the path.	35
"We went fishing on the dock," Ann says. "See what we got!"	47
Dad and Ann hold up fish.	53
"I like that," Mom says. "We can* have corn hash and fish for dinner.	67

- The target rate for **Getting Started** is 60 wcpm. The asterisks (*) mark 60 words.
- Listen to the student read the passage. Count the number of words read in one minute and the number of errors.
- For the reading rate, subtract the number of errors from the total number of words read.
- Have students enter their scores on their **Fluency Graph**. See page 9.

Answer Key

Building Background

Name _____ Date _____

Let's Go Camping
What You Know
Write answers to these questions.

1. What is something fun you and your family do? _____
   Answers will vary.

2. Think of two things you need to take with you if you go camping.
   Ideas: flashlight, bug repellent, food, sleeping bags,
   clothes, tent

Word Meanings
Definitions
Look for these words as you read your chapter book. When you find one of these words, write its definition.

dock: a long platform that is built over water as a landing place for ships or boats

eat: to put into the mouth, chew, and swallow

fire: the heat and light of something burning

hash: a finely chopped mixture

lake: a large body of water surrounded by land

look: to turn or aim one's eyes in order to see

Let's Go Camping — 12

Chapter Quiz

Name _____ Date _____

Let's Go Camping
Chapter 1, "Let's Go Camping"
Mark each statement *T* for true or *F* for false.

- **T** 1. There are four people in this family.
- **T** 2. Mom puts bags in the van.
- **F** 3. The dog's name is Ann.
- **F** 4. The dog is not going camping.
- **T** 5. They go north to the lake.

Read the question, and write your answer.

Why does Dad want to go camping? It is hot.

Let's Go Camping — 14

Chapter Quiz

Name _____ Date _____

Let's Go Camping
Chapter 2, "At the Camp"
Fill in the bubble beside the answer for each question.

1. Who sets up the tent?
   - Ⓐ Mom and Dad
   - Ⓑ Dad
   - ● Mom and Ann

2. A bug gets
   - Ⓐ Dad.
   - ● Ann.
   - Ⓒ Mom.

3. What does Dad want to do?
   - Ⓐ go for a walk
   - Ⓑ sleep
   - ● sit by the fire pit

Let's Go Camping — 15

Chapter Quiz

Name _____ Date _____

Let's Go Camping
Chapter 3, "The Path"
Number the events in order from 1 to 5.

- **2** Dad says, "We can go down the path."
- **4** Bud gets muddy.
- **5** Mom asks, "What did he do that for?"
- **1** Ann sees a path.
- **3** Bud rubs his neck in the mud.

Let's Go Camping — 16

Answer Key

Chapter Quiz

Name _____ Date _____

Let's Go Camping
Chapter 4, "Swimming"
Number the events in order from 1 to 5.

- **4** Bud slips on the dock.
- **1** Ann says, "Let's go swimming!"
- **2** Ann picks up a shell and puts it in her vest.
- **5** Bud swims to the shore.
- **3** Bud runs on the dock.

Read the question, and write your answer.

Why is Bud not muddy now? **He fell into the lake and the water cleaned the mud off.**

Let's Go Camping

Chapter Quiz

Name _____ Date _____

Let's Go Camping
Chapter 5, "Corn Hash"
Fill in the bubble beside the answer for each question.

1. Who went fishing?
   - Ⓐ Dad
   - ● Dad and Ann
   - Ⓒ Mom and Dad

2. Why don't they eat the ham?
   - Ⓐ It is not cooked.
   - Ⓑ Bud has eaten half of it already.
   - ● It has ants on it.

3. What does Mom make for dinner?
   - Ⓐ sandwiches
   - Ⓑ soup
   - ● corn hash

Read the question, and write your answer.

Who eats the ham? **Bud**

Let's Go Camping

Chapter Quiz

Name _____ Date _____

Let's Go Camping
Chapter 6, "Dinner at Last!"
Mark each statement *T* for true or *F* for false.

- **F** 1. Mom says it is okay to eat before Dad and Ann get back.
- **T** 2. Dad and Ann bring fish.
- **F** 3. The family eats ham and corn hash for dinner.
- **T** 4. The sun sets.
- **F** 5. The family did not have fun camping.

Let's Go Camping

Thinking and Writing

Name _____ Date _____

Let's Go Camping
Think About It
Write about or give an oral presentation for each question.

1. What part of this camping trip do you think was the most fun?
   Answers will vary.

2. What is a fun place you go with your family? Why is it fun?
   Answers will vary.

Write About It
Choose one of the questions below. Write your answer on a sheet of paper.

1. If you could take a trip anywhere, where would you go?
2. Complete the Sequencing Chart for this book.

Let's Go Camping

Getting Started • Book 1

Building Background

Name _____ Date _____

Baseball
What You Know

Write answers to these questions.

1. List some baseball teams. _____
   _____
   _____
   _____

2. How do you get a home run? _____
   _____
   _____
   _____

Word Meanings
Definitions

Look for these words as you read your chapter book. When you find one of these words, write its definition.

base: _____

batter: _____

mitt: _____

pitch: _____

team: _____

trot: _____

Word Lists

Baseball

Unfamiliar Words	Word Meanings	
field says	team	Chapter 1
are safe team	base	Chapter 2
first game home throws	pitch	Chapter 3
strike	batter	Chapter 4
from	trots	Chapter 5
catch	mitt	Chapter 6

Getting Started • Book 2

Chapter Quiz

Name _____ Date _____

Baseball
Chapter 1, "Play Ball!"

Fill in the bubble beside the answer for each question.

1. What does Sid hit?
   - Ⓐ the bat
   - Ⓑ the stick
   - Ⓒ the ball

2. How is the ball field?
   - Ⓐ muddy
   - Ⓑ dusty
   - Ⓒ small

3. What can Bud see?
   - Ⓐ Al and Sid play
   - Ⓑ his cap
   - Ⓒ the team

Chapter Quiz

Name _____ Date _____

Baseball
Chapter 2, "The Red Team"

Number the events in order from 1 to 5.

___ Sid swings the bat.

___ The ball hits Al's hands.

___ Sid sees the ball rushing to her.

___ Bud says a mitt will help.

___ Sid sits back.

Read the question, and write your answer.

Why are Al's hands sore? _____

_____

Chapter Quiz

Name _____ Date _____

Baseball
Chapter 3, "The Green Team"

Mark each statement *T* for true or *F* for false.

_____ 1. Sam and Sid sit in the field.

_____ 2. Kit is a fast runner.

_____ 3. Kit misses the ball.

_____ 4. Sid catches the ball.

_____ 5. Kit gets a home run.

Read the question, and write your answer.

Do you think the Red Team will win the next time they play? Why or why not? _____

_____

_____

Chapter Quiz

Name _____ Date _____

Baseball
Chapter 4, "The Tan Team"

Fill in the bubble beside the answer for each question.

1. The batter
   - Ⓐ hits the ball.
   - Ⓑ strikes out.
   - Ⓒ gets a home run.

2. What can Sid do?
   - Ⓐ pitch
   - Ⓑ catch
   - Ⓒ bat

3. Who wins?
   - Ⓐ the Tan Team
   - Ⓑ the Green Team
   - Ⓒ the Red Team

Read the question, and write your answer.

Does Sid pitch well? Why or why not? _____

_____

_____

_____

Getting Started • Book 2

Chapter Quiz

Name _____ Date _____

Baseball
Chapter 5, "Batter Up!"

Mark each statement *T* for true or *F* for false.

____ 1. Kit steps up to bat.

____ 2. Al sends a pitch to Kit.

____ 3. Kit hits the ball out of the field.

____ 4. Al kicks his feet in the grass.

____ 5. Sam hits the ball.

Read the question, and write your answer.

Does Sam want to bat? Why or why not? _____

_____

_____

Chapter Quiz

Name _____ Date _____

Baseball
Chapter 6, "The Winners"

Number the events in order from 1 to 5.

____ Sam gets a hit.

____ The Red Team wins.

____ Al runs home.

____ Al hits the ball.

____ Sid runs to first base.

Thinking and Writing

Name _____ Date _____

Baseball
Think About It

Write about or give an oral presentation for each question.

1. How do you think the Red Team feels when they lose to the Green Team? How do they feel when they win?

   _____

   _____

   _____

2. What does the Red Team do before they play the Green Team? Why?

   _____

   _____

   _____

Write About It

Choose one of the questions below. Write your answer on a sheet of paper.

1. Write about a game you play. What game is it? How do you play?

2. Complete the Sequencing Chart for this book.

Fluency Passages

Baseball

Chapter 2 *pages 6 and 7*

*Sid will bat next. She grips the bat. A ball jets by her.	13
Now Sid will hit. She swings the bat. The bat just clips the ball. Sam grabs the ball.	28 / 31
"Check how you are standing," Bud tells Sid. "Sit back. See the ball."	44
Sid sits back. The ball is fast. She sees it rushing to her.	57
Sid swings the* bat. *Crack!* The ball goes up and up.	68

Chapter 6 *page 26*

*Al checks how he is standing. He sits back. He sees the ball. It is rushing to him.	15 / 18
Al swings the bat. *Crack!* The ball goes up. It is rushing up, up, up.	33
Can the Green Team catch the ball? Hands go up. The ball drops in a mitt. Then it drops to the grass.	48 / 55
Sam runs home. Kit picks* up the ball.	63

- The target rate for **Getting Started** is 60 wcpm. The asterisks (*) mark 60 words.
- Listen to the student read the passage. Count the number of words read in one minute and the number of errors.
- For the reading rate, subtract the number of errors from the total number of words read.
- Have students enter their scores on their **Fluency Graph**. See page 9.

Answer Key

Building Background

Name _____ Date _____

Baseball
What You Know
Write answers to these questions.

1. List some baseball teams. **Ideas: New York Yankees, Los Angeles Dodgers, Chicago Cubs, St. Louis Cardinals, Atlanta Braves. Students may also name high school teams and teams the students themselves play on.**

2. How do you get a home run? **You get a home run by hitting the ball and running through first base, second base, third base, and finally to home plate without getting tagged out.**

Word Meanings
Definitions
Look for these words as you read your chapter book. When you find one of these words, write its definition.

base: **one of the four goals that a player must safely reach, one after the other, to score a run**
batter: **the player whose turn it is to bat**
mitt: **a large padded glove with a thumb but usually without separate fingers**
pitch: **to throw a ball to the batter**
team: **a group of people working together**
trot: **to run slowly with a loose, easy motion**

24 — Getting Started • Book 2 — *Baseball*

Chapter Quiz

Name _____ Date _____

Baseball
Chapter 1, "Play Ball!"
Fill in the bubble beside the answer for each question.

1. What does Sid hit?
   - Ⓐ the bat
   - Ⓑ the stick
   - ● the ball

2. How is the ball field?
   - Ⓐ muddy
   - ● dusty
   - Ⓒ small

3. What can Bud see?
   - ● Al and Sid play
   - Ⓑ his cap
   - Ⓒ the team

26 — Getting Started • Book 2 — *Baseball*

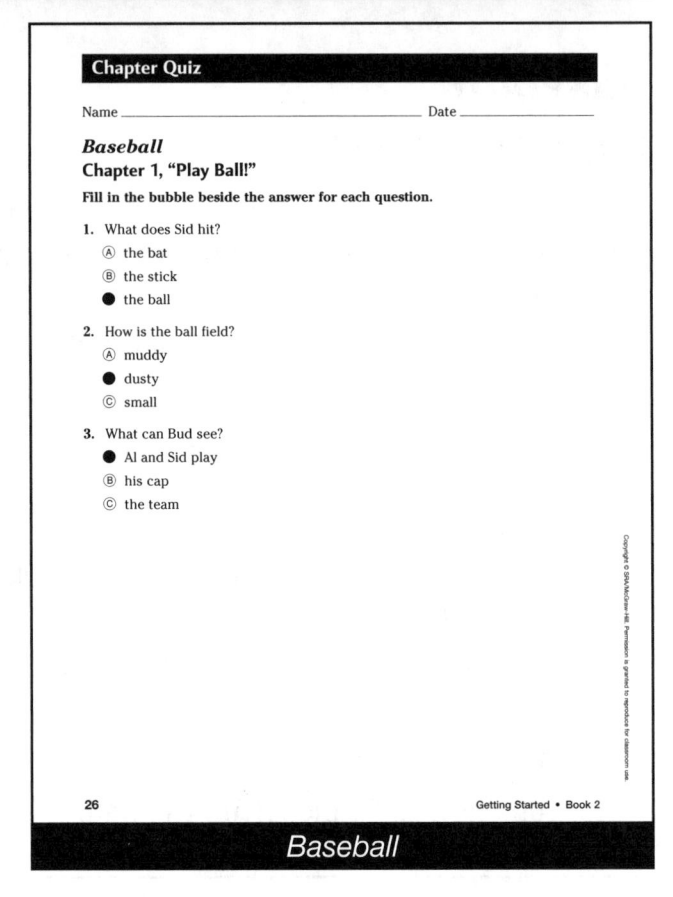

Chapter Quiz

Name _____ Date _____

Baseball
Chapter 2, "The Red Team"
Number the events in order from 1 to 5.

- **5** Sid swings the bat.
- **1** The ball hits Al's hands.
- **4** Sid sees the ball rushing to her.
- **2** Bud says a mitt will help.
- **3** Sid sits back.

Read the question, and write your answer.

Why are Al's hands sore? **Ideas: The ball hits Al's hands; Al needs a mitt.**

Getting Started • Book 2 — 27 — *Baseball*

Chapter Quiz

Name _____ Date _____

Baseball
Chapter 3, "The Green Team"
Mark each statement *T* for true or *F* for false.

- **F** 1. Sam and Sid sit in the field.
- **T** 2. Kit is a fast runner.
- **F** 3. Kit misses the ball.
- **F** 4. Sid catches the ball.
- **T** 5. Kit gets a home run.

Read the question, and write your answer.

Do you think the Red Team will win the next time they play? Why or why not? **Answers will vary.**

28 — Getting Started • Book 2 — *Baseball*

Answer Key

Chapter Quiz

Name _____ Date _____

Baseball
Chapter 4, "The Tan Team"
Fill in the bubble beside the answer for each question.

1. The batter
   - Ⓐ hits the ball.
   - ● strikes out.
   - Ⓒ gets a home run.

2. What can Sid do?
   - ● pitch
   - Ⓑ catch
   - Ⓒ bat

3. Who wins?
   - Ⓐ the Tan Team
   - Ⓑ the Green Team
   - ● the Red Team

Read the question, and write your answer.
Does Sid pitch well? Why or why not? **Sid pitches well. She strikes the batter out.**

Chapter Quiz

Name _____ Date _____

Baseball
Chapter 5, "Batter Up!"
Mark each statement *T* for true or *F* for false.

- **T** 1. Kit steps up to bat.
- **F** 2. Al sends a pitch to Kit.
- **T** 3. Kit hits the ball out of the field.
- **T** 4. Al kicks his feet in the grass.
- **F** 5. Sam hits the ball.

Read the question, and write your answer.
Does Sam want to bat? Why or why not? **Sam wants to bat. Sam wants to play the Green Team, and she wants to win.**

Chapter Quiz

Name _____ Date _____

Baseball
Chapter 6, "The Winners"
Number the events in order from 1 to 5.

- **1** Sam gets a hit.
- **5** The Red Team wins.
- **4** Al runs home.
- **3** Al hits the ball.
- **2** Sid runs to first base.

Thinking and Writing

Name _____ Date _____

Baseball
Think About It
Write about or give an oral presentation for each question.

1. How do you think the Red Team feels when they lose to the Green Team? How do they feel when they win?
   Ideas: The Red Team is unhappy when they lose to the Green Team. They feel happy when they win.

2. What does the Red Team do before they play the Green Team? Why?
   The Red Team practices before they play the Green Team. They practice so they can play well. If teams do not practice, they cannot win.

Write About It
Choose one of the questions below. Write your answer on a sheet of paper.

1. Write about a game you play. What game is it? How do you play?
2. Complete the Sequencing Chart for this book.

Getting Started • Book 2

Building Background

Name _____ Date _____

You Are Not Green
What You Know

Write answers to these questions.

1. What is a friend? _____
   _____
   _____

2. How do you make friends? _____
   _____
   _____

Word Meanings
Definitions

Look for these words as you read your chapter book. When you find one of these words, write its definition.

duck: _____

hawk: _____

pond: _____

sore: _____

where: _____

wing: _____

Word Lists

You Are Not Green

Unfamiliar Words	Word Meanings	
could, friends, look	duck	Chapter 1
find, flew, fly, too	hawk	Chapter 2
way	where	Chapter 3
past	pond	Chapter 4
where	wing	Chapter 5
fly	sore	Chapter 6

Chapter Quiz

Name _____ Date _____

You Are Not Green
Chapter 1, " 'No!' "

Mark each statement *T* for true or *F* for false.

____ 1. Frog wants friends that look like him.

____ 2. Duck does not need a friend.

____ 3. Frog needs Duck's help.

____ 4. Duck is happy.

____ 5. Duck wants to be like Frog.

Chapter Quiz

Name _____ Date _____

You Are Not Green
Chapter 2, "Hawk"

Number the events in order from 1 to 5.

_____ Hawk could not hold Frog.

_____ Frog hid by a rock.

_____ Hawk shot out of the sky and grabbed Frog.

_____ Frog hit rocks on a hill.

_____ Frog fell.

Read the question, and write your answer.

Why did Frog slip out of Hawk's grip? _____

_____

_____

Chapter Quiz

Name _____ Date _____

You Are Not Green
Chapter 3, "Lost!"

Fill in the bubble beside the answer for each question.

1. When Frog fell, what did Hawk do?
    - Ⓐ He looked for Frog.
    - Ⓑ He left Frog on the hill.
    - Ⓒ He flew back and grabbed Frog.

2. Why could Frog not hop fast?
    - Ⓐ His leg was sore.
    - Ⓑ He was lost.
    - Ⓒ He was hiding from Hawk.

3. Where did Frog sit down?
    - Ⓐ under a tree
    - Ⓑ under a rock
    - Ⓒ in the sun

Chapter Quiz

Name _____ Date _____

You Are Not Green
Chapter 4, "Duck Drops By"

Number the events in order from 1 to 5.

___ Duck flew down the hill to the pond.

___ Duck flew by and saw Frog.

___ Duck was sad as he flew back to the pond.

___ Duck did not bother Frog.

___ Duck said he was not green or cold.

Read the question, and write your answer.

Why did Duck feel sad as he flew back to the pond?

_____

_____

_____

Chapter Quiz

Name _____ Date _____

You Are Not Green
Chapter 5, "Where Is Frog?"

Fill in the bubble beside the answer for each question.

1. Who did Fish want to find?
   - Ⓐ Frog
   - Ⓑ Duck
   - Ⓒ Hawk

2. Why did Fish say Frog would get sick on the hill?
   - Ⓐ Frog must keep cold and wet.
   - Ⓑ The hill is too hot and sunny.
   - Ⓒ both A and B

3. Fish told Duck to
   - Ⓐ swim for help.
   - Ⓑ fly to Frog and wake him up.
   - Ⓒ fly fast and pick up Frog.

Chapter Quiz

Name _____ Date _____

You Are Not Green
Chapter 6, "Frog Can Fly"

Mark each statement *T* for true or *F* for false.

____ 1. When Duck flew to the tree, Frog was gone.

____ 2. Duck helped Frog hop back to the pond.

____ 3. Frog got in to the pond as fast as he could.

____ 4. Duck got in to the pond.

____ 5. Duck was still sad and wished he was green.

Read the question, and write your answer.

Why was Frog glad that Duck was not just like him?

_____

_____

_____

_____

Thinking and Writing

Name _____ Date _____

You Are Not Green
Think About It

Write about or give an oral presentation for each question.

1. How was Duck a good friend to Frog even when Frog would not be friends? _____
   _____
   _____

2. What did Frog find out about friends? _____
   _____
   _____
   _____

Write About It

Choose one of the questions below. Write your answer on a sheet of paper.

1. Write about one of your friends. Tell three ways you and your friend are alike. Tell three ways you and your friend are not alike. Tell why you are friends even when you are not alike.

2. Complete the Sequencing Chart for this book.

Fluency Passages

You Are Not Green

Chapter 4 *pages 18 and 19*

*"He is sleeping. I will not bother him now."	9
Duck felt sad as he flew back to the pond.	19
"I still wish I could be Frog's friend," he said. "But I am not green or	35
cold. Frogs can not be friends with ducks. Frog told me that.	47
"Still, how can Frog keep cold and wet in the sun? I must* ask him	62
when he gets back to the pond."	69

Chapter 6 *page 28*

*Frog got in to the pond as fast as he could.	11
"I feel much better now. You are my best friend, Duck!" Frog said. "I	25
am lucky that you are not just like me. I am lucky that you have wings!"	41
Duck got in to the pond with his friend. Duck was still not green or	56
cold, but he was* happy!	61

- The target rate for **Getting Started** is 60 wcpm. The asterisks (*) mark 60 words.
- Listen to the student read the passage. Count the number of words read in one minute and the number of errors.
- For the reading rate, subtract the number of errors from the total number of words read.
- Have students enter their scores on their **Fluency Graph**. See page 9.

Answer Key

Building Background

Name _____ **Date** _____

You Are Not Green
What You Know
Write answers to these questions.

1. What is a friend? **Answers will vary.**

2. How do you make friends? **Ideas: be nice to someone; help them; share with them**

Word Meanings
Definitions
Look for these words as you read your chapter book. When you find one of these words, write its definition.

duck: **a swimming bird that has a flat bill, short legs, and webbed feet**
hawk: **a large bird that has a strong, hooked beak and claws and has keen eyesight**
pond: **a small lake, often one that is man-made rather than natural**
sore: **aching or painful**
where: **at, in, or to what place**
wing: **one of a pair of parts covered with feathers that a bird spreads out from its sides in flying**

You Are Not Green

Chapter Quiz

Name _____ **Date** _____

You Are Not Green
Chapter 1, " 'No!' "
Mark each statement *T* for true or *F* for false.

T 1. Frog wants friends that look like him.
F 2. Duck does not need a friend.
F 3. Frog needs Duck's help.
F 4. Duck is happy.
T 5. Duck wants to be like Frog.

You Are Not Green

Chapter Quiz

Name _____ **Date** _____

You Are Not Green
Chapter 2, "Hawk"
Number the events in order from 1 to 5.

2 Hawk could not hold Frog.
5 Frog hid by a rock.
1 Hawk shot out of the sky and grabbed Frog.
4 Frog hit rocks on a hill.
3 Frog fell.

Read the question, and write your answer.
Why did Frog slip out of Hawk's grip? **Frog was too big for Hawk to carry.**

You Are Not Green

Chapter Quiz

Name _____ **Date** _____

You Are Not Green
Chapter 3, "Lost!"
Fill in the bubble beside the answer for each question.

1. When Frog fell, what did Hawk do?
   Ⓐ He looked for Frog.
   ● He left Frog on the hill.
   Ⓒ He flew back and grabbed Frog.

2. Why could Frog not hop fast?
   ● His leg was sore.
   Ⓑ He was lost.
   Ⓒ He was hiding from Hawk.

3. Where did Frog sit down?
   ● under a tree
   Ⓑ under a rock
   Ⓒ in the sun

You Are Not Green

Answer Key

Chapter Quiz

Name _____ Date _____

You Are Not Green
Chapter 4, "Duck Drops By"
Number the events in order from 1 to 5.

_5_ Duck flew down the hill to the pond.
_1_ Duck flew by and saw Frog.
_3_ Duck was sad as he flew back to the pond.
_2_ Duck did not bother Frog.
_4_ Duck said he was not green or cold.

Read the question, and write your answer.

Why did Duck feel sad as he flew back to the pond?
He still wanted to be Frog's friend.

Getting Started • Book 3 — 41

You Are Not Green

Chapter Quiz

Name _____ Date _____

You Are Not Green
Chapter 5, "Where Is Frog?"
Fill in the bubble beside the answer for each question.

1. Who did Fish want to find?
   ● Frog
   Ⓑ Duck
   Ⓒ Hawk

2. Why did Fish say Frog would get sick on the hill?
   Ⓐ Frog must keep cold and wet.
   Ⓑ The hill is too hot and sunny.
   ● both A and B

3. Fish told Duck to
   Ⓐ swim for help.
   Ⓑ fly to Frog and wake him up.
   ● fly fast and pick up Frog.

42 — Getting Started • Book 3

You Are Not Green

Chapter Quiz

Name _____ Date _____

You Are Not Green
Chapter 6, "Frog Can Fly"
Mark each statement *T* for true or *F* for false.

_F_ 1. When Duck flew to the tree, Frog was gone.
_F_ 2. Duck helped Frog hop back to the pond.
_T_ 3. Frog got in to the pond as fast as he could.
_T_ 4. Duck got in to the pond.
_F_ 5. Duck was still sad and wished he was green.

Read the question, and write your answer.

Why was Frog glad that Duck was not just like him?
Ideas: Duck had wings and Frog did not; Duck saved Frog because he flew Frog back to the pond.

Getting Started • Book 3 — 43

You Are Not Green

Thinking and Writing

Name _____ Date _____

You Are Not Green
Think About It
Write about or give an oral presentation for each question.

1. How was Duck a good friend to Frog even when Frog would not be friends? **Idea: He looked out for Frog, he wondered what was wrong, he found Frog, and he flew Frog back to the pond.**

2. What did Frog find out about friends? **Ideas: Friends do not have to be alike; sometimes being different can be very good; if Duck had not had wings, Frog would not have gotten back to the pond.**

Write About It
Choose one of the questions below. Write your answer on a sheet of paper.

1. Write about one of your friends. Tell three ways you and your friend are alike. Tell three ways you and your friend are not alike. Tell why you are friends even when you are not alike.

2. Complete the Sequencing Chart for this book.

44 — Getting Started • Book 3

You Are Not Green

Getting Started • Book 3 — 47

Building Background

Name _____ Date _____

The Pond
What You Know

Write answers to these questions.

1. What is a pond? Write your own definition. _____
   _____
   _____

2. What are some animals that live by ponds? _____
   _____
   _____

3. Begin the What I Know/What I Learned Chart for this book.

Word Meanings
Synonyms and Antonyms

Look for these words as you read your chapter book. When you find a word, write a synonym or antonym for the word.

Synonyms

bottom: _____

lay: _____

seek: _____

Antonyms

hot: _____

sit: _____

tiny: _____

Word Lists

The Pond

Unfamiliar Words	Word Meanings	
beavers, ducks, fly, live, water, where	bottom	Chapter 1
their, there, too, webbed	tiny	Chapter 2
eats, eggs, some	lay	Chapter 3
soon	sit	Chapter 4
	seek	Chapter 5
ice, spot	hot	Chapter 6

Getting Started • Book 4

Chapter Quiz

Name _____ Date _____

The Pond
Chapter 1, "At the Pond"

Number the events in order from 1 to 5.

____ The frog sings in the grass.

____ The ducks go down a hill.

____ Ducks fly north.

____ Frogs at the pond sing a greeting to the ducks.

____ A rat runs in the sand.

Read the question, and write your answer.

Which animals formed the pond? How? _____

_____

_____

_____

Chapter Quiz

Name _____ Date _____

The Pond
Chapter 2, "Fish and Beavers"

Fill in the bubble beside the answer for each question.

1. To help them swim, fish use
    - Ⓐ gills.
    - Ⓑ fins.
    - Ⓒ scales.

2. Where do the beavers live?
    - Ⓐ in the mud
    - Ⓑ in the reeds
    - Ⓒ under the dam

3. What is a kit?
    - Ⓐ a tiny beaver
    - Ⓑ a tiny fish
    - Ⓒ a water plant

Chapter Quiz

Name _____ Date _____

The Pond
Chapter 3, "Water Bugs and Frogs"

Mark each statement *T* for true or *F* for false.

____ 1. A water bug can swim on its back.

____ 2. The eggs of water bugs stick to plant stems.

____ 3. Frogs live only in the water.

____ 4. Frogs have webbed feet.

____ 5. Frogs eat plants.

Read the question, and write your answer.

Which animals eat frog eggs? _____

_____

Chapter Quiz

Name _____ Date _____

The Pond
Chapter 4, "Ducks and Ants"

Fill in the bubble beside the answer for each question.

1. What do ducks have to help them swim?
   - Ⓐ feathers
   - Ⓑ wings
   - Ⓒ webbed feet

2. Where are the ants digging a nest?
   - Ⓐ under a rock
   - Ⓑ on the sandy shore
   - Ⓒ in the grass

3. Where do ducks form nests?
   - Ⓐ in the water
   - Ⓑ in the grass
   - Ⓒ in a bush

Chapter Quiz

Name _____ Date _____

The Pond
Chapter 5, "Rats and More"

Mark each statement *T* for true or *F* for false.

_____ 1. Rats do not live at the pond.

_____ 2. Rats are born in the winter.

_____ 3. A rat can smell a clam in the sand.

_____ 4. Rats cannot swim.

_____ 5. Rats rest when the sun is up.

Chapter Quiz

Name _____ Date _____

The Pond
Chapter 6, "Ice on the Pond"

Number the events in order from 1 to 2.

____ The ducks fly to a spot where the sun is hot.

____ Ice forms on top of the water.

Mark each statement *T* for true or *F* for false.

____ 1. Water bugs and frogs sleep at the top of the pond.

____ 2. Fish rest under the ice.

____ 3. Ducks do not fly back in the spring.

Getting Started • Book 4

Thinking and Writing

Name _____ Date _____

The Pond
Think About It

Write about or give an oral presentation for each question.

1. What do you think the pond is like in the summer and fall?

   _____

   _____

2. Fish, bugs, frogs, and ducks all live by the pond and swim in it. What would you do by a pond?

   _____

   _____

Write About It

Choose one of the questions below. Write your answer on a sheet of paper.

1. Explain the difference between what life is like near a pond and what life is like near the ocean.

2. Complete the What I Know/What I Learned Chart for this book.

Fluency Passages

The Pond

Chapter 2 *page 7*

*Fish have no legs. They live in the pond water. Fish have fins to	14
help them swim.	17
Fish rub their fins in the mud at the bottom of the pond. They form	32
nests.	33
Fish feed on plants. Big fish feed on tiny fish too. A big fish swims	48
after a tiny fish. The tiny fish swims in to the water* plants. It swims fast.	64

Chapter 5 *pages 20 and 21*

*Tiny rats are born in the spring.	7
A clam is in its shell. It is sitting in the sand. A rat can smell the clam.	25
The rat digs for the clam. Then the rat eats it.	36
Rats are swimmers. They go in to the pond. They seek water bugs.	49
Rats feed on water bugs.	54
Rats swim under the water. They* seek fish. Rats feed on fish.	66

- The target rate for **Getting Started** is 60 wcpm. The asterisks (*) mark 60 words.

- Listen to the student read the passage. Count the number of words read in one minute and the number of errors.

- For the reading rate, subtract the number of errors from the total number of words read.

- Have students enter their scores on their **Fluency Graph**. See page 9.

Answer Key

Building Background

Name _____ Date _____

The Pond
What You Know

Write answers to these questions.

1. What is a pond? Write your own definition. _____
   Idea: A pond is a small area of water. It is bigger than a puddle but smaller than a lake.

2. What are some animals that live by ponds? _____
   Ideas: ducks, geese, dragonflies, frogs, toads

3. Begin the What I Know/What I Learned Chart for this book.

Word Meanings
Synonyms and Antonyms

Look for these words as you read your chapter book. When you find a word, write a synonym or antonym for the word.

Synonyms

bottom: **lowest part, floor**

lay: **put down, deposit**

seek: **search for, try to find**

Antonyms

hot: **cold, chilly**

sit: **stand**

tiny: **large, huge**

48 — Getting Started • Book 4 — *The Pond*

Chapter Quiz

Name _____ Date _____

The Pond
Chapter 1, "At the Pond"

Number the events in order from 1 to 5.

5 The frog sings in the grass.
3 The ducks go down a hill.
1 Ducks fly north.
2 Frogs at the pond sing a greeting to the ducks.
4 A rat runs in the sand.

Read the question, and write your answer.

Which animals formed the pond? How? **The beavers formed the pond. They cut down trees to make a dam; they put the trees in a creek; they rubbed mud on the trees to form a dam; the dam holds back the creek water; the water forms a pond.**

50 — Getting Started • Book 4 — *The Pond*

Chapter Quiz

Name _____ Date _____

The Pond
Chapter 2, "Fish and Beavers"

Fill in the bubble beside the answer for each question.

1. To help them swim, fish use
   Ⓐ gills.
   ● fins.
   Ⓒ scales.

2. Where do the beavers live?
   Ⓐ in the mud
   Ⓑ in the reeds
   ● under the dam

3. What is a kit?
   ● a tiny beaver
   Ⓑ a tiny fish
   Ⓒ a water plant

Getting Started • Book 4 — 51 — *The Pond*

Chapter Quiz

Name _____ Date _____

The Pond
Chapter 3, "Water Bugs and Frogs"

Mark each statement *T* for true or *F* for false.

T 1. A water bug can swim on its back.
T 2. The eggs of water bugs stick to plant stems.
F 3. Frogs live only in the water.
T 4. Frogs have webbed feet.
F 5. Frogs eat plants.

Read the question, and write your answer.

Which animals eat frog eggs? **water bugs and fish**

52 — Getting Started • Book 4 — *The Pond*

---

58 Getting Started • Book 4

Answer Key

Chapter Quiz

Name _____ Date _____

The Pond
Chapter 4, "Ducks and Ants"

Fill in the bubble beside the answer for each question.

1. What do ducks have to help them swim?
   - Ⓐ feathers
   - Ⓑ wings
   - ● webbed feet

2. Where are the ants digging a nest?
   - ● under a rock
   - Ⓑ on the sandy shore
   - Ⓒ in the grass

3. Where do ducks form nests?
   - Ⓐ in the water
   - ● in the grass
   - Ⓒ in a bush

The Pond

Chapter Quiz

Name _____ Date _____

The Pond
Chapter 5, "Rats and More"

Mark each statement *T* for true or *F* for false.

__F__ 1. Rats do not live at the pond.

__F__ 2. Rats are born in the winter.

__T__ 3. A rat can smell a clam in the sand.

__F__ 4. Rats cannot swim.

__T__ 5. Rats rest when the sun is up.

The Pond

Chapter Quiz

Name _____ Date _____

The Pond
Chapter 6, "Ice on the Pond"

Number the events in order from 1 to 2.

__1__ The ducks fly to a spot where the sun is hot.

__2__ Ice forms on top of the water.

Mark each statement *T* for true or *F* for false.

__F__ 1. Water bugs and frogs sleep at the top of the pond.

__T__ 2. Fish rest under the ice.

__F__ 3. Ducks do not fly back in the spring.

The Pond

Thinking and Writing

Name _____ Date _____

The Pond
Think About It

Write about or give an oral presentation for each question.

1. What do you think the pond is like in the summer and fall?
   Idea: In the summer, the baby animals grow; in the fall, the animals get ready for winter by collecting food.

2. Fish, bugs, frogs, and ducks all live by the pond and swim in it. What would you do by a pond?
   Ideas: swim; catch frogs; have a picnic

Write About It

Choose one of the questions below. Write your answer on a sheet of paper.

1. Explain the difference between what life is like near a pond and what life is like near the ocean.

2. Complete the What I Know/What I Learned Chart for this book.

The Pond

Getting Started • Book 4

Building Background

Name _____ Date _____

Freedom Morning
What You Know

Write answers to these questions.

1. Have you ever felt afraid of doing something even though it was an important thing to do? Write about that time.

   _____
   _____

2. Do you think it is ever okay to not tell the truth or to break rules? Explain your answer.

   _____
   _____

Word Meanings
Synonyms and Antonyms

Look for these words as you read your chapter book. When you find a word, write a synonym or antonym for the word.

Synonyms

hollow: _____

scared: _____

start: _____

Antonyms

bold: _____

open: _____

slow: _____

Word Lists

Freedom Morning

Unfamiliar Words	Word Meanings	Proper Nouns	
army, basket, eggs, freedom, girl, know, like, morning	hollow, scared	Mama, Sally	Scene 1
plans, put, south	slow	Mary Bowser, Miss Bet Van Lew, Mr. Davis	Scene 2
paper			Scene 3
walking	bold		Scene 4
guard, sir, walks	start	Mr. Wells	Scene 5
reads, woman	open		Scene 6

Getting Started • Book 5

Scene Quiz

Name _____ Date _____

Freedom Morning
Scene 1, "Go for Freedom"

Fill in the bubble beside the answer for each question.

1. Sally carries the eggs in a
   - Ⓐ basket.
   - Ⓑ carton.
   - Ⓒ sack.

2. What does Sally compare herself to?
   - Ⓐ a duck in the water
   - Ⓑ a fish in a lake
   - Ⓒ a frog in a pond

3. One egg in the basket is
   - Ⓐ brown.
   - Ⓑ broken.
   - Ⓒ hollow.

Read the question, and write your answer.

Why is Sally's mother scared? _____

_____

_____

Scene Quiz

Name _____ Date _____

Freedom Morning
Scene 2, "The Letter"

Mark each statement *T* for true or *F* for false.

_____ 1. Mary works for Mr. Davis.

_____ 2. Mr. Davis thinks Mary is smart.

_____ 3. Mary learns the plans of the Southern army by reading the mail.

_____ 4. The letter is not small enough to fit in an egg.

_____ 5. Mary thinks the letter will fit in an egg.

Read the question, and write your answer.

Other than the letter, how do Mary and Bet help the North?

_____

_____

_____

_____

Scene Quiz

Name _____ Date _____

Freedom Morning
Scene 3, "Go Well"

Number the events in order from 1 to 5.

____ Sally leaves to deliver the eggs.

____ Mary puts the letter in the hollow egg.

____ Sally comes to see Bet and Mary.

____ Bet offers Sally breakfast.

____ Sally hands the hollow egg to Bet.

Scene Quiz

Name _____ Date _____

Freedom Morning
Chapter 4, "The Street"

Mark each statement *T* for true or *F* for false.

____ 1. Sally talks to herself as she walks down the street.

____ 2. Sally delivers the letter because she cares about freedom.

____ 3. Sally is not scared.

____ 4. Sally's legs are like jelly.

____ 5. It is evening.

Scene Quiz

Name _____ Date _____

Freedom Morning
Chapter 5, "The Guard"

Mark each statement *T* for true or *F* for false.

____ 1. A guard stops Sally.

____ 2. Sally tells the guard she has eggs.

____ 3. The guard does not ask to see the basket.

____ 4. The guard lets Sally pick an egg for him.

____ 5. The guard tells Sally to go.

Read the question, and write your answer.

What do you think Sally was thinking when the guard was questioning her?

_____

_____

Scene Quiz

Name _____ Date _____

Freedom Morning
Chapter 6, "The Farm"

Fill in the bubble beside the answer for each question.

1. Why does the woman say she doesn't need Sally's eggs?
   - Ⓐ She doesn't like eggs.
   - Ⓑ She already got an egg delivery.
   - Ⓒ She lives on a farm.

2. The woman changes her mind because Sally says
   - Ⓐ Mr. Wells ordered the eggs.
   - Ⓑ Miss Van Lew sent the eggs.
   - Ⓒ the guard told her to bring the eggs.

3. Sally tells the man she delivered the eggs for
   - Ⓐ freedom.
   - Ⓑ money.
   - Ⓒ friendship.

Getting Started • Book 5

Thinking and Writing

Name _____ Date _____

Freedom Morning
Think About It

Write about or give an oral presentation for each question.

1. What did Sally risk losing to get the letter to the North?

   _____

   _____

   _____

2. What does a spy do? How is this different from what a soldier does?

   _____

   _____

   _____

Write About It

Choose one of the questions below. Write your answer on a sheet of paper.

1. What do you think would have happened if the guard who questioned Sally had chosen the hollow egg? Explain your thoughts in a paragraph.

2. Complete the Main Idea/Details Chart for this book.

Fluency Passages

Freedom Morning

Scene 1 *pages 1-3*

*It is morning. Mama is feeding the cat.	8
Mama: Sally!	10
Sally steps in. She has a basket of eggs.	19
Sally: Yes, Mama?	22
Mama: Do you have the basket?	28
Sally: Yes, Mama.	31
Mama: It is morning.	35
Sally: Yes. The sun is dim, but I can see it.	46
Mama: Are you cold?	50
Sally: No, Mama.	53
Mama: Sit by me.	57
Sally sits.	59
Mama:* How do you feel?	64

Scene 4 *pages 17-19*

Sally: Go on, Sally. Go on. You must not stop. What matters is the	15
letter. What matters is freedom.	19
You know this town. You know the streets. You know the stores. You can	33
not be scared of this old town.	40
But I am scared. My legs are like jelly. It is not cold, but I feel cold.	57
No! You will* be bold. The sun is up.	66

- The target rate for **Getting Started** is 60 wcpm. The asterisks (*) mark 60 words.
- Listen to the student read the passage. Count the number of words read in one minute and the number of errors.
- For the reading rate, subtract the number of errors from the total number of words read.
- Have students enter their scores on their **Fluency Graph**. See page 9.

Answer Key

Building Background

Name _____ Date _____

Freedom Morning
What You Know
Write answers to these questions.

1. Have you ever felt afraid of doing something even though it was an important thing to do? Write about that time.
   Answers will vary.

2. Do you think it is ever okay to not tell the truth or to break rules? Explain your answer.
   Accept reasonable responses.

Word Meanings
Synonyms and Antonyms
Look for these words as you read your chapter book. When you find a word, write a synonym or antonym for the word.

Synonyms
hollow: **empty, unfilled**
scared: **frightened, fearful**
start: **begin, commence**

Antonyms
bold: **timid, unadventurous**
open: **close, shut**
slow: **astute, bright**

Scene Quiz

Name _____ Date _____

Freedom Morning
Scene 1, "Go for Freedom"
Fill in the bubble beside the answer for each question.

1. Sally carries the eggs in a
   ● basket.
   Ⓑ carton.
   Ⓒ sack.

2. What does Sally compare herself to?
   Ⓐ a duck in the water
   Ⓑ a fish in a lake
   ● a frog in a pond

3. One egg in the basket is
   Ⓐ brown.
   Ⓑ broken.
   ● hollow.

Read the question, and write your answer.
Why is Sally's mother scared? **Idea: Sally's mother is worried that Sally will be caught by a Southern guard.**

Scene Quiz

Name _____ Date _____

Freedom Morning
Scene 2, "The Letter"
Mark each statement *T* for true or *F* for false.

T 1. Mary works for Mr. Davis.
F 2. Mr. Davis thinks Mary is smart.
F 3. Mary learns the plans of the Southern army by reading the mail.
F 4. The letter is not small enough to fit in an egg.
T 5. Mary thinks the letter will fit in an egg.

Read the question, and write your answer.
Other than the letter, how do Mary and Bet help the North?
Idea: Mary and Bet work as spies in Mr. Davis's house to gather information for the North.

Scene Quiz

Name _____ Date _____

Freedom Morning
Scene 3, "Go Well"
Number the events in order from 1 to 5.

5 Sally leaves to deliver the eggs.
4 Mary puts the letter in the hollow egg.
1 Sally comes to see Bet and Mary.
2 Bet offers Sally breakfast.
3 Sally hands the hollow egg to Bet.

Answer Key

Scene Quiz

Name _____ Date _____

Freedom Morning
Chapter 4, "The Street"
Mark each statement *T* for true or *F* for false.

- **T** 1. Sally talks to herself as she walks down the street.
- **T** 2. Sally delivers the letter because she cares about freedom.
- **F** 3. Sally is not scared.
- **T** 4. Sally's legs are like jelly.
- **F** 5. It is evening.

Getting Started • Book 5 65

Freedom Morning

Scene Quiz

Name _____ Date _____

Freedom Morning
Chapter 5, "The Guard"
Mark each statement *T* for true or *F* for false.

- **T** 1. A guard stops Sally.
- **T** 2. Sally tells the guard she has eggs.
- **F** 3. The guard does not ask to see the basket.
- **F** 4. The guard lets Sally pick an egg for him.
- **T** 5. The guard tells Sally to go.

Read the question, and write your answer.

What do you think Sally was thinking when the guard was questioning her?
Ideas: She was afraid because the guard might have chosen the hollow egg; she was afraid she would be caught.

66 *Getting Started • Book 5*

Freedom Morning

Scene Quiz

Name _____ Date _____

Freedom Morning
Chapter 6, "The Farm"
Fill in the bubble beside the answer for each question.

1. Why does the woman say she doesn't need Sally's eggs?
   - Ⓐ She doesn't like eggs.
   - Ⓑ She already got an egg delivery.
   - ● She lives on a farm.

2. The woman changes her mind because Sally says
   - Ⓐ Mr. Wells ordered the eggs.
   - ● Miss Van Lew sent the eggs.
   - Ⓒ the guard told her to bring the eggs.

3. Sally tells the man she delivered the eggs for
   - ● freedom.
   - Ⓑ money.
   - Ⓒ friendship.

Getting Started • Book 5 67

Freedom Morning

Thinking and Writing

Name _____ Date _____

Freedom Morning
Think About It
Write about or give an oral presentation for each question.

1. What did Sally risk losing to get the letter to the North?
   Idea: She risked her own safety.

2. What does a spy do? How is this different from what a soldier does?
   Ideas: Spies get secret information about the enemy and pass it to their allies; soldiers fight battles to defeat the enemy using information from the spies.

Write About It
Choose one of the questions below. Write your answer on a sheet of paper.

1. What do you think would have happened if the guard who questioned Sally had chosen the hollow egg? Explain your thoughts in a paragraph.

2. Complete the Main Idea/Details Chart for this book.

68 *Getting Started • Book 5*

Freedom Morning

Getting Started • Book 5   71

Building Background

Name _____ Date _____

The Fox and the Hen
What You Know

Write answers to these questions.

1. Do you have a talent or hobby? Write about it. _____
   _____
   _____

2. How has your talent or hobby helped you or someone else?
   _____
   _____

Word Meanings
Definitions

Look for these words as you read your chapter book. When you find one of these words, write its definition.

again: _____

boil: _____

fire: _____

mend: _____

round: _____

sew: _____

Word Lists

The Fox and the Hen

Unfamiliar Words	Word Meanings	
door looks says water	mend sew	Chapter 1
eat opens	boil	Chapter 2
ouch	round	Chapter 3
where	fire	Chapter 4
over try	again	Chapter 5
		Chapter 6

Getting Started • Book 6

Chapter Quiz

Name _____ Date _____

The Fox and the Hen
Chapter 1, "Hen"

Fill in the bubble beside the answer for each question.

1. What is Hen's hobby?
   - Ⓐ cooking
   - Ⓑ sewing
   - Ⓒ farming

2. Hen helps the animals by
   - Ⓐ mending their socks.
   - Ⓑ cooking dinner for them.
   - Ⓒ harvesting the corn.

3. Hen picks up
   - Ⓐ a stick.
   - Ⓑ a sock.
   - Ⓒ a rock.

Chapter Quiz

Name _____ Date _____

The Fox and the Hen
Chapter 2, "Fox"

Mark each statement *T* for true or *F* for false.

____ 1. Fox plans to eat Hen for dinner.

____ 2. Fox hides behind Hen's clock.

____ 3. Fox jumps out of the box.

____ 4. Hen locks the door.

____ 5. Hen lands on the rug.

Read the question, and write your answer.

What is Fox trying to do? _____

_____

Chapter Quiz

Name _____ Date _____

The Fox and the Hen
Chapter 3, "Will Fox Get Hen?"

Number the events in order from 1 to 5.

____ Hen falls.

____ Fox puts Hen in a sack.

____ Fox runs round and round.

____ Hen feels sick.

____ Fox grips Hen by her legs.

Chapter Quiz

Name _____ Date _____

The Fox and the Hen
Chapter 4, "Can Hen Stop Fox?"

Mark each statement *T* for true or *F* for false.

_____ 1. Fox carries the sack back to the den without stopping.

_____ 2. Hen escapes from the sack.

_____ 3. Hen puts a rock in the sack.

_____ 4. Hen sews up the sack.

_____ 5. Fox catches Hen again.

Read the question, and write your answer.

What words would you use to describe Hen and why? What words would you use to describe Fox and why?

_____

_____

_____

_____

Getting Started • Book 6

Chapter Quiz

Name _____ Date _____

The Fox and the Hen
Chapter 5, "Dinner"

Mark each statement *T* for true or *F* for false.

____ 1. Fox returns to the den with the sack.

____ 2. Fox and his mom eat corn for dinner.

Number the events in order from 1 to 3.

____ Fox is burned by the boiling water.

____ Fox dumps the rock into the pot.

____ Fox goes to the creek and gets a tub of cold water.

Read the question, and write your answer.

What does Fox learn in this story? _____

_____

_____

Chapter Quiz

Name _____ Date _____

The Fox and the Hen
Chapter 6, "Hen Again"

Fill in the bubble beside the answer for each question.

1. What does Sheep tell Hen?
   - Ⓐ Fox is hiding in the box.
   - Ⓑ Fox is packing to move away.
   - Ⓒ Fox and his mom feel sick.

2. Hen believes she
   - Ⓐ still has to worry about Fox.
   - Ⓑ will not see Fox again.
   - Ⓒ needs to buy a new door lock.

3. What does Hen make for Ram and Sheep?
   - Ⓐ hot water
   - Ⓑ a pot of corn
   - Ⓒ fox stew

Thinking and Writing

Name _____ Date _____

The Fox and the Hen
Think About It

Write about or give an oral presentation for each question.

1. Why are Fox and Hen good choices for the characters?

   _____

   _____

   _____

   _____

Write About It

Choose one of the questions below. Write your answer on a sheet of paper.

1. Fox and Hen both play tricks on one another. Write about a trick you played on someone. Tell who was there, where it happened, what happened, and why you played the trick.

2. Think of two other animals that could have been used to portray the main characters in this story. Explain why they would be good choices.

3. Complete the Story Grammar Map for this book.

Fluency Passages

The Fox and the Hen

Chapter 1 *pages 1-3*

*Hen can sew. She gets her kit. Hen pins a hem. Now she will sew	15
the hem. Next she will sew a sash.	23
Hen can mend. She will mend a bunch of socks. She will mend socks	37
for Sheep. She will mend socks for Ram. But will she mend a sock for Fox?	53
Fox is on the hill. Fox looks* down at Hen.	63

Chapter 5 *page 21*

*Mom Fox steps up to the pot and opens the lid. She has a fork in her	17
hand. Fox steps up to the pot. He opens the sack. He tips the sack.	32
Ding! The rock slams in to the pot. Hot water is rushing up. The hot pot	48
boils over. Hot water runs down the pot. It gets on Fox* and his mom.	63

- The target rate for **Getting Started** is 60 wcpm. The asterisks (*) mark 60 words.
- Listen to the student read the passage. Count the number of words read in one minute and the number of errors.
- For the reading rate, subtract the number of errors from the total number of words read.
- Have students enter their scores on their **Fluency Graph**. See page 9.

Answer Key

Building Background

Name _____ Date _____

The Fox and the Hen
What You Know
Write answers to these questions.

1. Do you have a talent or hobby? Write about it. _____
   Accept reasonable responses.
   _____

2. How has your talent or hobby helped you or someone else?
   Accept reasonable responses.
   _____

Word Meanings
Definitions
Look for these words as you read your chapter book. When you find one of these words, write its definition.

again: **once more**
boil: **to heat a liquid until it bubbles up and becomes steam**
fire: **something burning in a furnace, stove, or fireplace**
mend: **to repair or fix**
round: **shaped like a ball, a circle, or a tube**
sew: **to work, mend, or fasten with a needle and thread**

72 — Getting Started • Book 6

The Fox and the Hen

Chapter Quiz

Name _____ Date _____

The Fox and the Hen
Chapter 1, "Hen"
Fill in the bubble beside the answer for each question.

1. What is Hen's hobby?
   Ⓐ cooking
   ● sewing
   Ⓒ farming

2. Hen helps the animals by
   ● mending their socks.
   Ⓑ cooking dinner for them.
   Ⓒ harvesting the corn.

3. Hen picks up
   ● a stick.
   Ⓑ a sock.
   Ⓒ a rock.

74 — Getting Started • Book 6

The Fox and the Hen

Chapter Quiz

Name _____ Date _____

The Fox and the Hen
Chapter 2, "Fox"
Mark each statement *T* for true or *F* for false.

__T__ 1. Fox plans to eat Hen for dinner.
__F__ 2. Fox hides behind Hen's clock.
__T__ 3. Fox jumps out of the box.
__T__ 4. Hen locks the door.
__F__ 5. Hen lands on the rug.

Read the question, and write your answer.
What is Fox trying to do? **Fox is trying to catch Hen.**

Getting Started • Book 6 — 75

The Fox and the Hen

Chapter Quiz

Name _____ Date _____

The Fox and the Hen
Chapter 3, "Will Fox Get Hen?"
Number the events in order from 1 to 5.

__3__ Hen falls.
__5__ Fox puts Hen in a sack.
__1__ Fox runs round and round.
__2__ Hen feels sick.
__4__ Fox grips Hen by her legs.

76 — Getting Started • Book 6

The Fox and the Hen

Answer Key

Chapter Quiz

Name _____ Date _____

The Fox and the Hen
Chapter 4, "Can Hen Stop Fox?"

Mark each statement *T* for true or *F* for false.

- **F** 1. Fox carries the sack back to the den without stopping.
- **T** 2. Hen escapes from the sack.
- **T** 3. Hen puts a rock in the sack.
- **T** 4. Hen sews up the sack.
- **F** 5. Fox catches Hen again.

Read the question, and write your answer.

What words would you use to describe Hen and why? What words would you use to describe Fox and why?
Ideas: Hen is clever because she uses her sewing kit to escape and puts the rock in the sack so Fox won't know about her escape. Fox is overconfident because he stops to take a nap.

Getting Started • Book 6   77

The Fox and the Hen

Chapter Quiz

Name _____ Date _____

The Fox and the Hen
Chapter 5, "Dinner"

Mark each statement *T* for true or *F* for false.

- **T** 1. Fox returns to the den with the sack.
- **F** 2. Fox and his mom eat corn for dinner.

Number the events in order from 1 to 3.

- **2** Fox is burned by the boiling water.
- **1** Fox dumps the rock into the pot.
- **3** Fox goes to the creek and gets a tub of cold water.

Read the question, and write your answer.

What does Fox learn in this story? **Idea: Fox learns that treating others badly will cause him harm.**

78   Getting Started • Book 6

The Fox and the Hen

Chapter Quiz

Name _____ Date _____

The Fox and the Hen
Chapter 6, "Hen Again"

Fill in the bubble beside the answer for each question.

1. What does Sheep tell Hen?
   - Ⓐ Fox is hiding in the box.
   - Ⓑ Fox is packing to move away.
   - ● Fox and his mom feel sick.

2. Hen believes she
   - Ⓐ still has to worry about Fox.
   - ● will not see Fox again.
   - Ⓒ needs to buy a new door lock.

3. What does Hen make for Ram and Sheep?
   - Ⓐ hot water
   - ● a pot of corn
   - Ⓒ fox stew

Getting Started • Book 6   79

The Fox and the Hen

Thinking and Writing

Name _____ Date _____

The Fox and the Hen
Think About It

Write about or give an oral presentation for each question.

1. Why are Fox and Hen good choices for the characters?
   Ideas: There is a natural conflict between foxes and hens; people think of foxes as being greedy, tricky, or clever and hens as silly or not smart.

Write About It

Choose one of the questions below. Write your answer on a sheet of paper.

1. Fox and Hen both play tricks on one another. Write about a trick you played on someone. Tell who was there, where it happened, what happened, and why you played the trick.

2. Think of two other animals that could have been used to portray the main characters in this story. Explain why they would be good choices.

3. Complete the Story Grammar Map for this book.

80   Getting Started • Book 6

The Fox and the Hen

Getting Started • Book 6   83

Building Background

Name _____ Date _____

The Farm
What You Know

Write answers to these questions.

1. What is on a farm? _____
   _____

2. Where do eggs come from? _____
   _____

Word Meanings
Definitions

Look for these words as you read your chapter book. When you find one of these words, write its definition.

barn: _____

egg: _____

food: _____

hay: _____

milk: _____

wool: _____

Word Lists

The Farm

Unfamiliar Words	Word Meanings	
animals boy from	barn	Chapter 1
warm water	food	Chapter 2
cows make work	milk	Chapter 3
fall	wool	Chapter 4
girl nose pull wagon	hay	Chapter 5
lay too	eggs	Chapter 6

Getting Started • Book 7

Chapter Quiz

Name _____ Date _____

The Farm
Chapter 1, "At the Farm"

Fill in the bubble beside the answer for each question.

1. The farm has
   - Ⓐ a big lake.
   - Ⓑ a lot of land.
   - Ⓒ no trees.

2. What does Dad plant?
   - Ⓐ corn
   - Ⓑ small trees
   - Ⓒ green grass

3. The farm is
   - Ⓐ not fun.
   - Ⓑ a lot of fun.
   - Ⓒ kind of fun.

Read the question, and write your answer.

What animals are on the farm? _____

_____

Chapter Quiz

Name _____ Date _____

The Farm
Chapter 2, "Pigs"

Mark each statement *T* for true or *F* for false.

____ 1. Dad has slop for the pigs.

____ 2. The slop is made of corn and peel and crust.

____ 3. The pigs do not need water.

____ 4. The boy has water for the pigs.

____ 5. Dad will sell the pigs in town.

Chapter Quiz

Name _____ Date _____

The Farm
Chapter 3, "Cows"

Mark each statement *T* for true or *F* for false.

____ 1. When the cows get big, they will go to town in the truck.

____ 2. An ox is a big sheep.

____ 3. The cows feed on bags of corn.

____ 4. Farm hands milk the cows.

____ 5. The farm hands have eggs for lunch.

Read the question, and write your answer.

When do the farm hands milk the cows? _____

_____

Chapter Quiz

Name _____ Date _____

The Farm
Chapter 4, "Sheep"

Fill in the bubble beside the answer for each question.

1. The farm hand
   - Ⓐ flips the sheep on to a block.
   - Ⓑ puts the sheep in the truck.
   - Ⓒ clips the sheep dog.

2. The sheep dog
   - Ⓐ runs down to the creek.
   - Ⓑ kicks its legs.
   - Ⓒ runs after the sheep.

3. In the spring
   - Ⓐ the farm hand will clip the ram.
   - Ⓑ the black sheep will go to town in the truck.
   - Ⓒ more sheep will be born.

Chapter Quiz

Name _____ Date _____

The Farm
Chapter 5, "The Horse"

Mark each statement *T* for true or *F* for false.

____ 1. The horse will have a colt.

____ 2. The colt drops to the hay.

____ 3. The colt stands before the horse licks it.

____ 4. The girl will not take care of the horse and the colt.

____ 5. The boy and the girl will go on the hay wagon.

Read the question, and write your answer.

Why is the vet in the barn? _____

_____

_____

Chapter Quiz

Name _____ Date _____

The Farm
Chapter 6, "The Hen"

Fill in the bubble beside the answer for each question.

1. A hen
   - Ⓐ is at the barn.
   - Ⓑ feeds on corn and seeds.
   - Ⓒ flaps and hops.

2. When the sun is down,
   - Ⓐ the girl gets eggs from under the hen.
   - Ⓑ the hen will go in the shack.
   - Ⓒ the hen feeds on corn and seeds.

3. Chicks will become
   - Ⓐ colts.
   - Ⓑ cows.
   - Ⓒ hens.

Thinking and Writing

Name _____ Date _____

The Farm
Think About It

Write about or give an oral presentation for each question.

1. Why does Dad plant corn? _____
   _____
   _____

2. What things does Dad sell? Why? _____
   _____
   _____

Write About It

Choose one of the questions below. Write your answer on a sheet of paper.

1. Pretend you live on a farm. What job would you want to do on the farm?

2. Complete the Content Web for this book.

Fluency Passages

The Farm

Chapter 4 *pages 18 and 19*

*The sheep kicks its legs. It runs to the end of the pen. The sheep dog 16
runs after it. The sheep runs down to the creek. It feeds on the grass. 31

The ram is at the creek. It had its wool clipped. The ram jumps on the 47
rocks. It drinks water from the creek. 54

A black sheep is at the* creek. It has black wool. 65

Chapter 6 *page 26*

*A hen is at the farm. She feeds on corn and seeds. The hen flaps and 16
runs. Her feet make tracks in the sand. 24

When the sun sets, the hen will go in the shack. She sits on her eggs 40
to keep them warm. 44

In the morning, the girl gets eggs from under the hen. Mom will feed 58
eggs to* the farm hands. 63

- The target rate for **Getting Started** is 60 wcpm. The asterisks (*) mark 60 words.
- Listen to the student read the passage. Count the number of words read in one minute and the number of errors.
- For the reading rate, subtract the number of errors from the total number of words read.
- Have students enter their scores on their **Fluency Graph**. See page 9.

Answer Key

Building Background

Name _____ Date _____

The Farm
What You Know
Write answers to these questions.

1. What is on a farm? **Accept reasonable responses.**

2. Where do eggs come from? **Idea: Among chickens, the hens lay eggs.**

Word Meanings
Definitions
Look for these words as you read your chapter book. When you find one of these words, write its definition.

barn: **a building for sheltering cows and other animals and for storing farm machines and crops**

egg: **the oval or round object that is laid by a female bird**

food: **anything that is taken in by a plant or animal to keep up its life and growth**

hay: **grass, clover, and other similar plants that have been cut and dried for feeding animals**

milk: **a white liquid formed in special glands of female mammals for feeding their young**

wool: **the soft, curly hair of sheep**

84 — Getting Started • Book 7

The Farm

Chapter Quiz

Name _____ Date _____

The Farm
Chapter 1, "At the Farm"
Fill in the bubble beside the answer for each question.

1. The farm has
   - Ⓐ a big lake.
   - ● a lot of land.
   - Ⓒ no trees.

2. What does Dad plant?
   - ● corn
   - Ⓑ small trees
   - Ⓒ green grass

3. The farm is
   - Ⓐ not fun.
   - ● a lot of fun.
   - Ⓒ kind of fun.

Read the question, and write your answer.

What animals are on the farm? **hen, pig, sheep, horse, dog**

86 — Getting Started • Book 7

The Farm

Chapter Quiz

Name _____ Date _____

The Farm
Chapter 2, "Pigs"
Mark each statement *T* for true or *F* for false.

F 1. Dad has slop for the pigs.
T 2. The slop is made of corn and peel and crust.
F 3. The pigs do not need water.
T 4. The boy has water for the pigs.
T 5. Dad will sell the pigs in town.

Getting Started • Book 7 — 87

The Farm

Chapter Quiz

Name _____ Date _____

The Farm
Chapter 3, "Cows"
Mark each statement *T* for true or *F* for false.

T 1. When the cows get big, they will go to town in the truck.
F 2. An ox is a big sheep.
T 3. The cows feed on bags of corn.
T 4. Farm hands milk the cows.
F 5. The farm hands have eggs for lunch.

Read the question, and write your answer.

When do the farm hands milk the cows? **in the morning and after dinner**

88 — Getting Started • Book 7

The Farm

Answer Key

Chapter Quiz

Name _____ Date _____

The Farm
Chapter 4, "Sheep"
Fill in the bubble beside the answer for each question.

1. The farm hand
   - ● flips the sheep on to a block.
   - Ⓑ puts the sheep in the truck.
   - Ⓒ clips the sheep dog.

2. The sheep dog
   - Ⓐ runs down to the creek.
   - Ⓑ kicks its legs.
   - ● runs after the sheep.

3. In the spring
   - Ⓐ the farm hand will clip the ram.
   - Ⓑ the black sheep will go to town in the truck.
   - ● more sheep will be born.

Chapter Quiz

Name _____ Date _____

The Farm
Chapter 5, "The Horse"
Mark each statement *T* for true or *F* for false.

__T__ 1. The horse will have a colt.
__T__ 2. The colt drops to the hay.
__F__ 3. The colt stands before the horse licks it.
__F__ 4. The girl will not take care of the horse and the colt.
__T__ 5. The boy and the girl will go on the hay wagon.

Read the question, and write your answer.
Why is the vet in the barn? **The vet will help the horse have a colt.**

Chapter Quiz

Name _____ Date _____

The Farm
Chapter 6, "The Hen"
Fill in the bubble beside the answer for each question.

1. A hen
   - Ⓐ is at the barn.
   - ● feeds on corn and seeds.
   - Ⓒ flaps and hops.

2. When the sun is down,
   - Ⓐ the girl gets eggs from under the hen.
   - ● the hen will go in the shack.
   - Ⓒ the hen feeds on corn and seeds.

3. Chicks will become
   - Ⓐ colts.
   - Ⓑ cows.
   - ● hens.

Thinking and Writing

Name _____ Date _____

The Farm
Think About It
Write about or give an oral presentation for each question.

1. Why does Dad plant corn? **Idea: The cows and hens eat corn.**

2. What things does Dad sell? Why? **Dad sells cows, pigs, and eggs. Dad can use the money to buy things.**

Write About It
Choose one of the questions below. Write your answer on a sheet of paper.

1. Pretend you live on a farm. What job would you want to do on the farm?
2. Complete the Content Web for this book.

Getting Started • Book 7   95

Building Background

Name _____ Date _____

Log Cabin Help
What You Know

Write answers to these questions.

1. What is a log cabin? _____

2. Have you gone to bed when there was no snow and then awakened to snow in the morning? Tell about it.
   _____
   _____

3. What is a sled? What time of the year do people ride sleds?
   _____
   _____

Word Meanings
Definitions

Look for these words as you read your chapter book. When you find one of these words, write its definition.

cabin: _____

gash: _____

mitts: _____

read: _____

snow: _____

steep: _____

Word Lists

Log Cabin Help

Unfamiliar Words	Word Meanings	
school	cabin	Chapter 1
fire says	read	Chapter 2
food from	snow	Chapter 3
pull	mitts	Chapter 4
	steep gash	Chapter 5
		Chapter 6

Getting Started • Book 8   97

Chapter Quiz

Name _____ Date _____

Log Cabin Help
Chapter 1, "On the Path to the School"

Fill in the bubble beside the answer for each question.

1. Ann, Ted, and Dan go to the
   - Ⓐ log cabin.
   - Ⓑ school.
   - Ⓒ store.

2. Ted and Dan
   - Ⓐ go slow.
   - Ⓑ are tall.
   - Ⓒ are big.

3. Ann needs
   - Ⓐ her hat.
   - Ⓑ to get to the log cabin.
   - Ⓒ Dan and Ted to help her.

Read the question, and write your answer.

Ann could not see Dan and Ted. Where were they?

_____

_____

_____

Chapter Quiz

Name _____ Date _____

Log Cabin Help
Chapter 2, "At the School"

Number the events in order from 1 to 3.

____ Dan and Ted add a log to the fire.

____ Ted and Dan get to the school.

____ Ann gets to the school.

Mark each statement *T* for true or *F* for false.

____ 1. Ann checks maps.

____ 2. The fire warms Ann.

Read the question, and write your answer.

Where do Ted and Dan sit? _____
_____

Chapter Quiz

Name _____ Date _____

Log Cabin Help
Chapter 3, "Dinner at the Log Cabin"

Mark each statement *T* for true or *F* for false.

_____ 1. Ann helps Mom get the food on the dish.

_____ 2. Mom and Ann cut and mash.

_____ 3. Ted and Dan do not step in to the log cabin with Dad.

_____ 4. Mom doesn't mend Ann's hem.

_____ 5. Dad says it will snow.

Read the question, and write your answer.

How do Dan and Ted help? _____

_____

Chapter Quiz

Name _____ Date _____

Log Cabin Help
Chapter 4, "To the School in the Snow"

Fill in the bubble beside the answer for each question.

1. How does Ann get to the school?
   - Ⓐ She sits on the sled.
   - Ⓑ She runs with Dan and Ted.
   - Ⓒ She walks with Dan and Ted.

2. At the school,
   - Ⓐ Dan and Ted help Ann.
   - Ⓑ Ann drops her ink pen.
   - Ⓒ Miss Green helps Ann.

3. After lunch Miss Green
   - Ⓐ helps Ann get her ink pen.
   - Ⓑ says they must go home.
   - Ⓒ helps Ann get her cap and mitts.

Chapter Quiz

Name _____ Date _____

Log Cabin Help
Chapter 5, "The Steep Hill"

Mark each statement *T* for true or *F* for false.

_____ 1. Ann gets her cap and her mitts.

_____ 2. The snow is not deep.

_____ 3. Ted and Ann tramp in the snow to get the sled.

_____ 4. Ted and the sled rush down the hill.

_____ 5. Ted helps Ann get back on the sled.

Read the question, and write your answer.

How did Ted get a gash on his leg? _____
_____

Chapter Quiz

Name _____ Date _____

Log Cabin Help
Chapter 6, "Ted Gets Better"

Fill in the bubble beside the answer for each question.

1. Dan gets
   - Ⓐ mad at Ted.
   - Ⓑ a hot drink.
   - Ⓒ the sled back to the log cabin.

2. What does Ann do?
   - Ⓐ She helps Dad and Mom.
   - Ⓑ She helps Ted get in bed.
   - Ⓒ She helps Dan get a log for the fire.

3. When Ted gets better
   - Ⓐ he can go back to the school.
   - Ⓑ he will fix the sled.
   - Ⓒ Dad will take him to the school.

Thinking and Writing

Name _____ Date _____

Log Cabin Help
Think About It

Write about or give an oral presentation for each question.

1. Why does Dad think it will snow? _____
   _____
   _____
   _____

2. Why do you think Dan wants to trap a fox? _____
   _____
   _____
   _____

Write About It

Choose one of the questions below. Write your answer on a sheet of paper.

1. What good things can go on in a school if big kids are with smaller kids?

2. Complete the Story Grammar Map for this book.

Fluency Passages

Log Cabin Help

Chapter 1 *pages 1 and 2*

 *Ann, Ted, and Dan have left the log cabin. Now they go to the school.   14 / 15

 Ted and Dan are big. They go fast. Ann can not go as fast.   29

 Ann runs down the path to the school. She trips on a stump. Then she steps on her hem. She must get to the school.   43 / 54

 It is cold. Ann grips her* hat. She needs Dan and Ted to help her.   69

Chapter 5 *page 20*

 *Ann gets her cap and her mitts. Dan and Ted tramp in the snow to get the sled. Ann sits on the sled. It is cold. The snow is deep.   15 / 30

 "We can go up the steep hill," Ted says. "The sled will go so fast."   45

 They go up the steep hill. Ann gets up. Ted sits on the sled. Ted* and the sled rush down the hill.   60 / 67

- The target rate for **Getting Started** is 60 wcpm. The asterisks (*) mark 60 words.
- Listen to the student read the passage. Count the number of words read in one minute and the number of errors.
- For the reading rate, subtract the number of errors from the total number of words read.
- Have students enter their scores on their **Fluency Graph**. See page 9.

Answer Key

Building Background

Name _____ Date _____

Log Cabin Help
What You Know
Write answers to these questions.

1. What is a log cabin? **A log cabin is a house made with logs.**

2. Have you gone to bed when there was no snow and then awakened to snow in the morning? Tell about it.
   Answers will vary.

3. What is a sled? What time of the year do people ride sleds?
   A sled is a platform that slides in the snow. People ride sleds in winter.

Word Meanings
Definitions
Look for these words as you read your chapter book. When you find one of these words, write its definition.

cabin: **a small house that is built in a simple, rough way, usually out of wood**

gash: **a long, deep cut**

mitts: **a glove with one pouch for the thumb and a larger pouch for the four fingers**

read: **to get the meaning of something written or printed by understanding its letters, signs, or numbers**

snow: **soft, white flakes that form from tiny drops of water that freeze in the upper air and fall to the earth**

steep: **having a sharp slant up or down**

Log Cabin Help

Chapter Quiz

Name _____ Date _____

Log Cabin Help
Chapter 1, "On the Path to the School"
Fill in the bubble beside the answer for each question.

1. Ann, Ted, and Dan go to the
   Ⓐ log cabin.
   ● school.
   Ⓒ store.

2. Ted and Dan
   Ⓐ go slow.
   Ⓑ are tall.
   ● are big.

3. Ann needs
   Ⓐ her hat.
   Ⓑ to get to the log cabin.
   ● Dan and Ted to help her.

Read the question, and write your answer.
Ann could not see Dan and Ted. Where were they?
Dan and Ted ran faster than Ann. They were far ahead.

Log Cabin Help

Chapter Quiz

Name _____ Date _____

Log Cabin Help
Chapter 2, "At the School"
Number the events in order from 1 to 3.

3 Dan and Ted add a log to the fire.
1 Ted and Dan get to the school.
2 Ann gets to the school.

Mark each statement *T* for true or *F* for false.
F 1. Ann checks maps.
T 2. The fire warms Ann.

Read the question, and write your answer.
Where do Ted and Dan sit? **They sit in desks in the back of the school.**

Log Cabin Help

Chapter Quiz

Name _____ Date _____

Log Cabin Help
Chapter 3, "Dinner at the Log Cabin"
Mark each statement *T* for true or *F* for false.

T 1. Ann helps Mom get the food on the dish.
T 2. Mom and Ann cut and mash.
F 3. Ted and Dan do not step in to the log cabin with Dad.
F 4. Mom doesn't mend Ann's hem.
T 5. Dad says it will snow.

Read the question, and write your answer.
How do Dan and Ted help? **Dan can fix things and set traps. Ted can chop wood.**

Log Cabin Help

106   Getting Started • Book 8

Answer Key

Chapter Quiz

Name _____ Date _____

Log Cabin Help
Chapter 4, "To the School in the Snow"
Fill in the bubble beside the answer for each question.

1. How does Ann get to the school?
   - ● She sits on the sled.
   - Ⓑ She runs with Dan and Ted.
   - Ⓒ She walks with Dan and Ted.

2. At the school,
   - Ⓐ Dan and Ted help Ann.
   - Ⓑ Ann drops her ink pen.
   - ● Miss Green helps Ann.

3. After lunch Miss Green
   - Ⓐ helps Ann get her ink pen.
   - ● says they must go home.
   - Ⓒ helps Ann get her cap and mitts.

Chapter Quiz

Name _____ Date _____

Log Cabin Help
Chapter 5, "The Steep Hill"
Mark each statement *T* for true or *F* for false.

__T__ 1. Ann gets her cap and her mitts.
__F__ 2. The snow is not deep.
__F__ 3. Ted and Ann tramp in the snow to get the sled.
__T__ 4. Ted and the sled rush down the hill.
__F__ 5. Ted helps Ann get back on the sled.

Read the question, and write your answer.

How did Ted get a gash on his leg? __Ted went down the hill fast on the sled and crashed in to a tree.__

Chapter Quiz

Name _____ Date _____

Log Cabin Help
Chapter 6, "Ted Gets Better"
Fill in the bubble beside the answer for each question.

1. Dan gets
   - Ⓐ mad at Ted.
   - Ⓑ a hot drink.
   - ● the sled back to the log cabin.

2. What does Ann do?
   - ● She helps Dad and Mom.
   - Ⓑ She helps Ted get in bed.
   - Ⓒ She helps Dan get a log for the fire.

3. When Ted gets better
   - ● he can go back to the school.
   - Ⓑ he will fix the sled.
   - Ⓒ Dad will take him to the school.

Thinking and Writing

Name _____ Date _____

Log Cabin Help
Think About It
Write about or give an oral presentation for each question.

1. Why does Dad think it will snow? __They have a north wind. That will make it colder.__

2. Why do you think Dan wants to trap a fox? __Idea: Dan may have chickens, a cat, or a small dog the fox would try to eat.__

Write About It
Choose one of the questions below. Write your answer on a sheet of paper.

1. What good things can go on in a school if big kids are with smaller kids?
2. Complete the Story Grammar Map for this book.

Getting Started • Book 8   107

Graphic Organizer

Name _____ Date _____

Let's Go Camping
Sequencing Chart

List steps or events in time order (in the order they occurred in the story).

Topic:
First:
Next:
Next:
Next:
Next:
Next:
Next:
Finally:

Graphic Organizer

Name _____ Date _____

Baseball
Sequencing Chart

List steps or events in time order (in the order they occurred in the story).

Topic:
First:
Next:
Next:
Next:
Next:
Next:
Next:
Finally:

Getting Started

Graphic Organizer

Name _____ Date _____

You Are Not Green
Sequencing Chart

List steps or events in time order (in the order they occurred in the story).

Topic:
First:
Next:
Next:
Next:
Next:
Next:
Next:
Finally:

Name _____ Date _____

The Pond
What I Know/What I Learned Chart

What I Know	What I Want to Know	What I Learned

Getting Started

Graphic Organizer

Name _____ Date _____

Freedom Morning
Main Idea/Details Chart

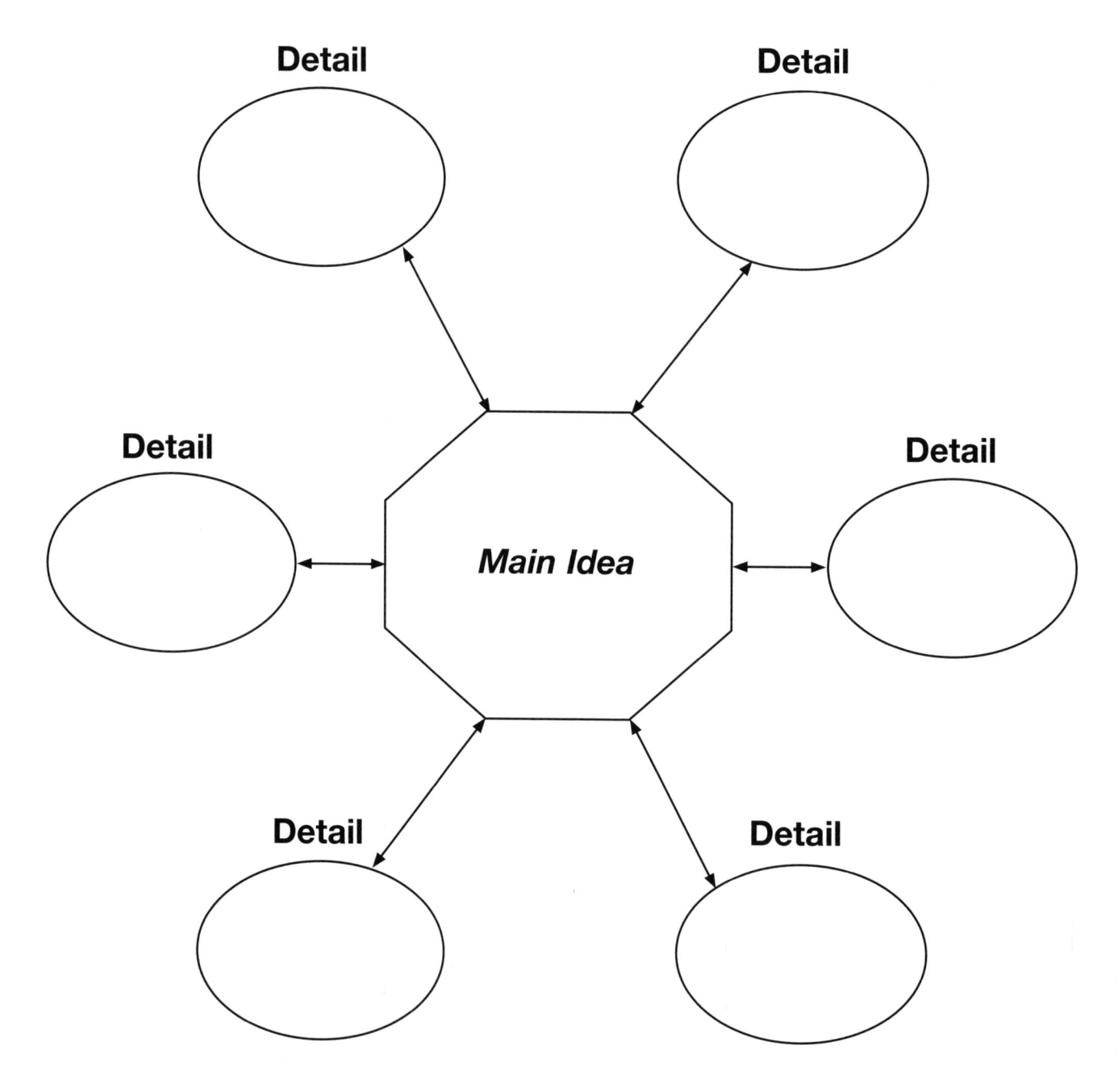

- Detail
- Detail
- Detail
- Main Idea
- Detail
- Detail
- Detail

Getting Started

Graphic Organizer

Name _____ Date _____

The Fox and the Hen
Story Grammar Map

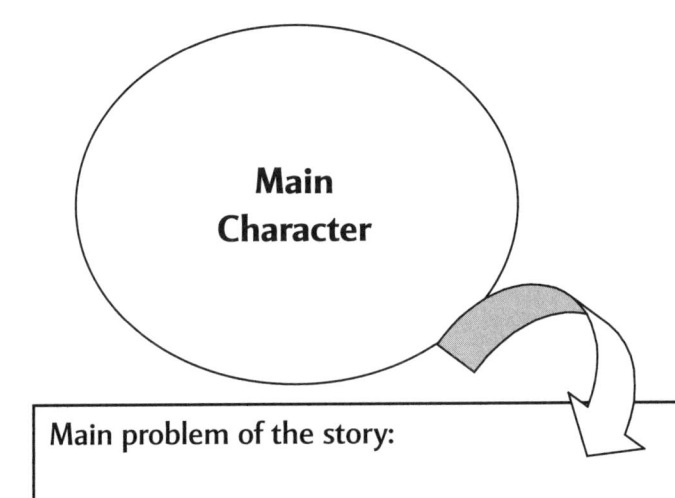

Main Character

Setting

Main problem of the story:

An event in the story:

An event in the story:

How was the story's problem solved?

What is the ending?

Graphic Organizer

Name _____ Date _____

The Farm
Content Web

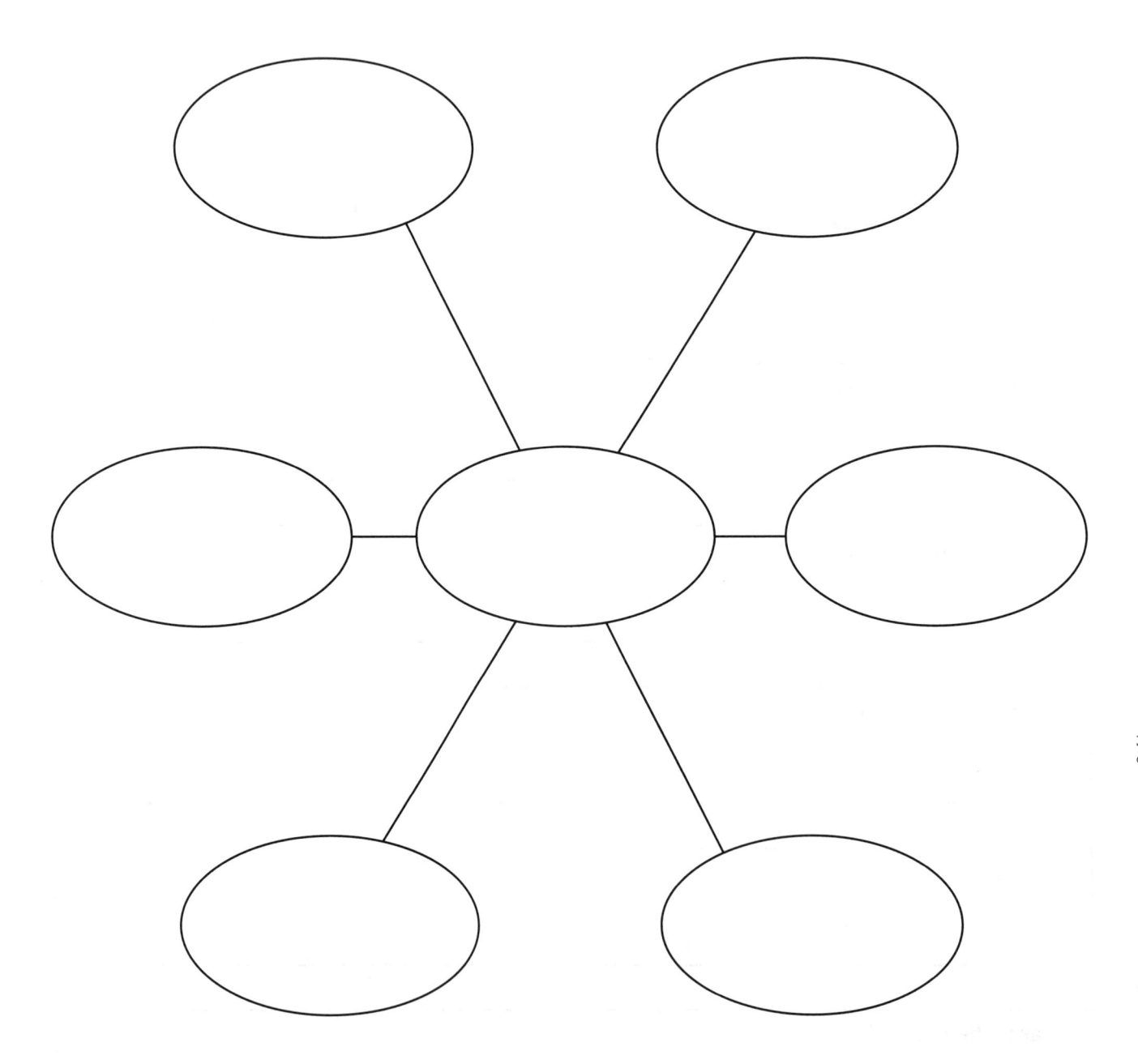

114 Getting Started

Graphic Organizer

Name _____ Date _____

Log Cabin Help
Story Grammar Map

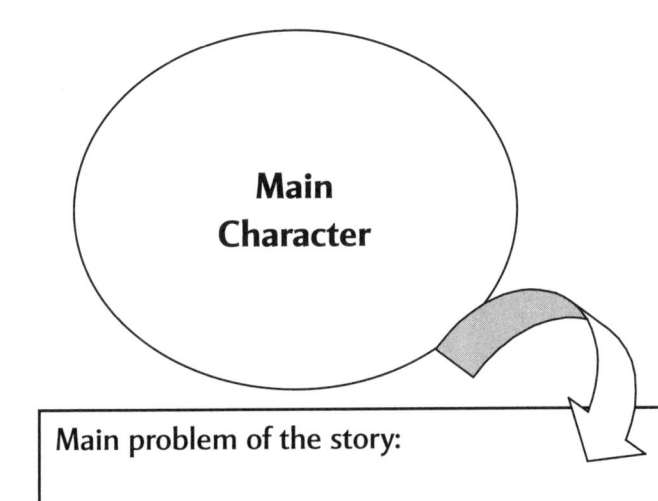

Main Character

Setting

Main problem of the story:

An event in the story:

An event in the story:

How was the story's problem solved?

What is the ending?